My Journey Home

Life after the Holocaust

My Journey Home

Life after the Holocaust

ZSUZSANNA OZSVÁTH

BOSTON
2019

ISBN 9781618119001 (hardcover)
ISBN 9781618119025 (ebook)
ISBN 9781618119018 (paperback)
©Academic Studies Press, 2019

Book design by Lapiz Digital Services

Published by Cherry Orchard Books, imprint of Academic Studies Press.
28 Montfern Avenue
Brighton, MA 02135, USA
press@academicstudiespress.com
www.academicstudiespress.com

Library of Congress Cataloging-in-Publication Data
Names: Ozsváth, Zsuzsanna, 1931- author.
Title: My journey home : life after the Holocaust / Zsuzsanna Ozsváth.
Description: Boston : Academic Studies Press, 2019.
Identifiers: LCCN 2018054910 (print) | LCCN 2018056189 (ebook) | ISBN
  9781618119025 (ebook) | ISBN 9781618119001 (hardcover) | ISBN 9781618119018
  (pbk.)
Subjects: LCSH: Ozsváth, Zsuzsanna, 1931- |
  Jews–Hungary–Budapest–Biography. | Jews, Hungarian–United
  States–Biography. | Holocaust survivors–Biography. | Budapest
  (Hungary)–Biography.
Classification: LCC DS135.H93 (ebook) | LCC DS135.H93 O976 2019 (print) | DDC
  940.53/18092 [B] –dc23
LC record available at https://lccn.loc.gov/2018054910

Acknowledgements

I would like to express my thanks to many people and institutions for their help and support in the preparation of this book. First of all, I would like to mention my deeply felt gratitude to Dr. Hobson Wildenthal, whose encouragement and interest in our work has been indispensable to the creation of the Holocaust Studies Program at UT Dallas. In addition, I would like to thank Dr. Dennis Kratz, Dean of the School of Arts and Humanities, for his encouragement and support. Also, I am deeply grateful to Mimi and Mitch Barnett, endowing the Leah and Paul Lewis Chair of Holocaust Studies at UT Dallas, for their extraordinary help and interest in my work and for the contribution of the Lewis Chair to my publication costs. In addition, I am indebted to Cricket Roemer, Gerri Patterson, and Martha Satz for both their friendships and invaluable comments. At the same time, I would like to express my deepest gratitude to my beloved colleagues, Nils Roemer and David Patterson for their friendship and the mark they have put on my research as well. This book is dedicated to my daughter, Kathleen, my son, Peter, his wife, Shevi, and to our five grandchildren, Elizabeth, Eliana, Tamar, Nina, and Leora.

Contents

Acknowledgements v
Foreword: *Hobson Wildenthal* ix

1. Spring Meeting 1
2. Promise of the Night 8
3. Encountering Pista 11
4. In the Garden 18
5. The First Visit 22
6. The Rise of Terror 24
7. Fear 31
8. Hunger 33
9. The Wedding 36
10. Shadows and Light 39
11. The Railed Cot 43
12. Quiet Happiness 45
13. Under Terror 47
14. Living for the Moment 56
15. Playmates 61
16. Dangerous Winds 67
17. Deportations 71
18. A Decision 73
19. Voyage to the East 76
20. New Circumstances 79
21. Across the Border 88

22. New Life	90
23. Waiting for a Miracle	93
24. Hamburg	98
25. First Steps	100
26. Crisis	108
27. Major Changes	117
28. New Life	119
29. A Terrible Event	124
30. Becoming Parents	126
31. Pleasure and Grief	128
32. At Home	133
33. Teaching and Fulfillment	142
34. Past and Present	146
35. Threats	149
36. The Crush of the World	151
37. Life with and without Pista	158
Index	162

Foreword

I wish I could read this new book of Zsuzsi's again, experiencing it as a stranger who did not know the protagonists or even whether they actually existed, a reader uninformed about whether the story was "true" or was a work of fiction. How would I react to this complex fairy tale, a tale incorporating all of the terror and sadness of the darkest of the Brothers Grimm's fantasies along with the happiest, most improbably sweet resolutions that either fiction or the real world allows. How would I react to the portraits of the protagonists? That they are archetypes too extreme for realistic fiction, let alone real life? Or that their vivid singularities are in fact evidence of an unvarnished reality? Or are they an author's highly sophisticated avoidance of the too plausible "averageness" of typical fictional characters?

I wish I could read and react to this story in the state of mind of the ignorant and naïve twenty-year-old product of small-town Texas that I was sixty years ago. How different would the reaction of my mind then have been from that of my mind now, as it has evolved over the intervening sixty years, marinated in a steady reading of fiction and history treating on the engagements of America and Americans with Europe and Europeans, and our drastically different experiences of the twentieth century. And even more important than my readings, those sixty years led me to residence in Europe and deep and intense involvements with contemporaries from the "old world" whose lives before our encounters had been as different from mine as if we had grown up in alternate universes.

All this is to say, the reactions I experienced in reading Zsuzsanna Ozsváth's memoir left me asking myself continuously for the reason that it was resonating with me so strongly. Was it the essence of the story? Was it the technique with which it was being told? Or was it just me and my own particular life history? Obviously, one can never read a story with a mind blank of knowledge and memory. But, since Zsuzsi's recounting of her life after World War II intersected so strongly with my own personal propensities, I continue to wonder how differently-conditioned minds will react to this true story that is literally "stranger than fiction," peopled by characters whose inner and outer emotional and intellectual lives are revealed with uniquely direct and intense transparency. One leaves this book knowing Zsuzsi and Pista much more deeply than before, even after twenty-plus years of professional and personal friendship. One finishes the book knowing them better than one knows almost anyone else, even one's closest friends and family. Likewise, after finishing the book, one has the feeling of understanding the experiences of European friends who lived through the varying traumas of World War II and its aftermath more clearly than was ever achieved though countless hours of personal conversations.

I met Zsuzsanna "Zsuzsi" Ozsváth and István "Pista" Ozsváth soon after I arrived at the University of Texas at Dallas in 1992. I cannot remember precisely those initial encounters now, nor whether I met them separately as two different faculty scholars or as a couple. What did I learn about them from our first meeting until this late-in-life reading of her memoir?

Pista was immediately easy for me to place as one of the founding members, along with his friends and colleagues Ivor Robinson and Wolfgang Rindler of the university's famous "relativity group." Along with similarly small groups of internationally distinguished scholars in molecular biology, space physics, and geophysics, the "relativity" group constituted the scientific staff recruited at the creation of the Graduate Research Center of the Southwest, the private research center that evolved into UT Dallas. These faculty groups set the standards of excellence and eminence that created the DNA inherited by and still manifested at the university.

Pista was the quiet one of the relativity trio—in absolute terms, not just "relatively." One might have thought that he just did not want to compete with Ivor's carefully crafted and resonantly flamboyant rhetoric, honed in his native England, or with Wolfgang's urbane, suave, and witty anecdotes recounted in his own elegant English accent, acquired in his case after his arrival in England as an adolescent "*Kindertransport*" refugee. Pista's German-influenced, Hungarian-accented English was delightfully not pol-ished in England but rather hard won after his arrival in Texas. I believe his son told the story of his acquiring one of his languages in emergency conditions by immersing himself in popular television programs.

However, Pista's taciturnity was in no way because he was shy or inhib-ited. He was simply not inclined to talk just to hear himself. He was always ready with the summarizing *mot juste* at the end of others' lengthy expo-sitions. In any case, however many languages Pista spoke and understood, it was clear to everyone that his true language was mathematics. Since the relativity group needed and desired little from the provost other than respect and non-interference, and I was happy to oblige, I did not have not have much direct contact with Pista in his role as faculty member through the intervening years.

What I intuited about Pista was that he had found the absolutely perfect environment and perfect career niche for his inclinations and talents. He appeared in some ways to be the ultimate example of the abstracted, head-in-the-clouds professor, although in Pista's case it was the cosmos, not the clouds, where his mind and spirit resided. (Another story, told lovingly, was that at more intellectually intense times in his lectures he would occasionally lapse from English into German.) At the same time, his close friends knew he possessed the deeply grounded personal confidence and practicality of the peasant boy who had worked the family farm in rural Hungary, comfortable in and on the soil.

But personally, I came to know Pista mostly as Zsuzsi's husband and head of family. They seemed a perfectly complementary pair in every way: Pista a bulwark of calm, common sense, and master of his profession and of the house, Zsuzsi the extroverted, charismatic artist-intellectual with a mission of altering the trajectory of society. I worked closely with Zsuzsi in those early years of the 1990s, impressed and intrigued by her success in having created and kept alive a small program focusing on study of and education about the Holocaust. Of course, almost everything about UT Dallas was small in those days, but Zsuzsi had secured some endowments, had some distinguished Dallas citizens sitting on her advisory board, and was bringing to campus some internationally distinguished personages as speakers.

I became more and more involved with her as we attempted to gain more community support for her program, and I urged her to think expansively about what we might do with her creation in terms of new events, programs, people, and facilities. With the stimulus of Zsuzsi's energetic commitment to advancing her program, and my engagement with her visitors and community friends that grew out of my support, I found myself becoming an amateur scholar of the Holocaust myself, a project of late-life self-education that grew into a deeply enriching new dimension of my thinking. This is the background of my two decades of friendship with Pista and Zsuzsi: convivial and stimulating dinners in their home with visitors, meeting their children and old friends, sharing books and ideas, learning incrementally more about their past lives, and growing ever more admiration for the lives and careers they had built in Dallas. I learned something of Zsuzsi's passion for music; her intensely patriotic *Sehnsucht* about the

Hungary that was dismembered at the Trianon Conference (I had to go look that up); and her passionate, deeply analytical devotion to her teaching and her mission. Finally, I grew to understand the fanatical devotion she engendered in her students, formal and informal.

Today, Zsuzsi and I are getting old, and we look back with some satisfaction about what has been accomplished at UT Dallas with our Holocaust Studies Program, now endowed as the Ackerman Center. We have lost Pista, but Zsuzsi carries on with incredible courage and energy. And now, she has followed our urgings and has "written it down." What has her story told us about these two immensely talented individuals whose life partnership seemed in the eyes of the world a perfect example of the attraction of opposites? To me, Zsuzsi's story validates everything we thought about the Ozsváths but expands for us what was, relatively speaking, a charcoal sketch of their lives into a three-dimensional Technicolor production with sound and music. All of our perceptions were true, but at the same time we were quite uncomprehending of the depths of passion, love, despair, fear, survival, escape, homesickness, frustration, and ultimately a sort of triumph that marked our friends' inner lives. Zsuzsi tells a story of love at first sight, love never ending, and a lifetime of an almost perfect union between two souls so different and yet maybe not so different at the deepest level, souls unquestionably perfectly matched. And she tells it with an artless art that lets us view into those souls with a singularly powerful clarity.

Dr. Hobson Wildenthal,
Executive Vice President at UT Dallas

1

Spring Meeting

I met István in Budapest on the first of May, 1949. Opening the shutters that morning, I saw the sun sparkling high up in the azure sky and noticed the trees and flowers just starting to bloom. Suddenly I remembered the great event waiting for me at the end of the day, and I was filled with delight and happy expectation. Sure, I knew that now I had to hurry up, get dressed, and run to my school's May Day festivities, running from early morning until late afternoon, a "celebration" which was forced upon us by the Communist Party and which angered me to no end. But afterwards—and at this thought my heart raced, and I took a deep breath—afterwards, I was to visit my friend Kati Fischmann, who had invited me to a party with six young mathematicians. Three of them, she told me, were second-year classmates of hers in the mathematics department at the Péter Pázmány University of Budapest; the other three had enrolled in the same program but were one year younger. She couldn't wait, she said, for all of us to come together that evening so we could forget about the unpleasant celebration of the day and have a good time together. In fact, she remarked, we would make fun of the threats, the senseless rules and regulations by which we had been forced to glorify the "leadership of the Soviet Union, and the great, free world of the Party's working class"—in short, the lies and cruel tyranny of the Communist government of Hungary.

I was ready for this night. In fact for the past two weeks, the thought of being invited to Kati's house had made me feel happy. First of all, I had never been invited to a "grown-up" party before, with so many young men; second, I had always yearned for great conversations with people and was very much looking forward to this opportunity. In addition, I was excited because even the thought of this party at Kati's helped me overcome my impatience and anger at the unpleasant mass celebrations we had been forced to attend during the day.

I was seventeen years old and knew only a few young men outside the musical profession. I practiced piano day and night, hoping to become a concert pianist. Most of my young colleagues were doing the same: they played a large variety of musical instruments, and all hoped to become famous performers. Of course, some had already had passionate love affairs. But not me. I had never had any experience of that kind—except when I was ten and in love with my piano teacher, the famous young pianist György Faragó. He died of pancreatic cancer during the Siege of Budapest. But that was, of course, years before I came to understand that my feelings for him were connected to my dedication to music and his heartbreakingly beautiful playing as well as to his heroic help in saving our lives and those of other people during the German occupation of Hungary. As I look back to that time, I see that my love for him may be described as a child's admiration for the fairy-tale prince who came to save her and her family from the evil dragon attempting to slay them.

I had left school when I was twelve years old and took my yearly exams as a homeschooled student. I practiced six to eight hours a day and took classes first at the Music Academy and later at the Béla Bartók Music Conservatory. I also loved literature and was still deeply preoccupied with the Holocaust—then four years past, yet very much present in my life. Despite the fact that in 1945 the Russian army had saved our lives when it liberated Hungary, by the late forties I had begun to recognize the nature of the Soviet-led Communist Party in Hungary with its threats, exclusions, and arrests of large numbers of people, even people I knew to be longtime members and true supporters of the Communist cause.

The Communist Party had been established in Hungary in 1918 when Béla Kun, a former journalist, returned from Moscow to Hungary. Instrumental to the creation of the Hungarian Soviet Republic in March 1919, Kun embarked on both the nationalization of private property and the collectivization of agriculture. His government was defeated by Miklós Horthy and the invading Romanian troops; Kun was exiled to Vienna. It was at this point that the fighters of the White Terror, a new rightist movement under the leadership of Horthy, initiated the imprisonment and torture of thousands of people in Hungary. In the meantime, the major leaders of the Hungarian Communist Party fled to Moscow. Many of them were later accused of treason, including Kun, and were killed during Stalin's purges. The arbitrary murder of the so-called "enemies" of Hungary didn't stop after World War II, however: it continued during the second half of the

1940s until Stalin's death in 1953. By then, most Hungarians had become aware of the power of the new terror that started to dominate their lives. During this period, tens of thousands of people were imprisoned, fifteen thousand deported, and more than five thousand killed in a country of fewer than ten million people.

As for today, everybody was forced under the threat of punishment to participate in the May Day celebration. I, too, felt I must go ahead. Angry and bored by what I knew was waiting for me at the parade, I was overjoyed by the thought of Kati's party. In her company, I knew I would forget the annoying events of the day and be introduced to and have wonderful discussions with six—yes, six—highly intelligent and impressive young mathematicians.

*　*　*

Of course, the huge parades planned by the Communist parties of the Soviet bloc for the first of May event were not devised for a "joyful celebration of the population," as it was officially emphasized, nor were they invented to "raise the consciousness of the workers in the fight against the capitalistic regimes of the world," as the media repeatedly reported. Rather, these goals were forced upon the countries occupied by the Soviet Union and ruled by their own Communist governments. Originally commemorated as International Workers' Day, the first of May was now an occasion for celebrating the leadership of the Soviet Union in countries that had become part of the "Soviet interest zone" after World War II. Indeed, following the practice of the Soviet Republic, the Communist governments of Eastern and Central Europe demanded that on this day their populations participate in organized street demonstrations and march to celebrate the victory of the Soviet army during World War II, as formulated by their own national Communist propaganda. All official descriptions professed their admiration for "the Great Stalin, the Soviet Union, and its leadership among the nations of the world." The festivities included gigantic military displays. In addition to showing countless pictures and statues of Stalin, people in Hungary had to exalt the president of the Council of Ministers, István Dobi, and the secretary general of the Communist Party, Mátyás Rákosi.

This was, of course, no coincidence. By 1949 Hungary, the small, Russian-occupied country in Central Europe that had fought on the side of Germany during both world wars, was ruled by its newly revived Communist Party and received directions directly from Moscow. For one of the outcomes of the Treaty of Yalta was that the Allies gave into Stalin's demand and, like several other countries of Eastern and Central Europe, Hungary found itself in the Soviet interest zone, hopelessly cut off from the rest of Europe and from the rest of the world. This development had wide-ranging political consequences: while Hungary's democratic coalition government, created immediately after World War II, made every attempt to take its first steps toward democracy, its goals had been wiped away by the "higher goals" of the Soviet Union. Communication between the East and the West collapsed. And since Stalin demanded that the countries occupied by the Soviet army during World War II maintain a tight relationship with Moscow, escape was not possible. The growing Soviet terror intensified in Eastern Europe. Hungary had no means of resisting. As a result, by 1949 the brutal reign of terror overshadowed everyday life and eradicated all hope for freedom. The well-organized May Day parade was just a manifestation of the Soviet Union's overwhelming power. Workers in Budapest and in every town and village—hundreds of thousands of them—were ordered to participate in the May Day celebrations and display their firm belief in the Party, Hungary's Communist government, and the Soviet Union.

To organize such a huge celebration was, of course, not easy. On the first of May, 1949, near Budapest's City Park, gigantic crowds searched for their assigned places—at times successfully, at others quite hopelessly. Workers, tradespeople, and professionals—including clerks and a large variety of state employees from nationalized businesses, factories, offices, and firms—gathered together with students, teachers, and professors of the various schools and academic institutions. They were ordered by the Communist leadership of their institutions to unite for the occasion. Hundreds of thousands of people in Budapest marched on this order, moving back and forth in the streets. Every factory, workplace, school, and department had its own supervisor who checked off arrivals from a list. Under these circumstances, the consequences of staying at home would have been dire. The ready-made lists had to be checked while people waited in line so that the presence or absence of individuals whose names were on record could easily be ascertained. Offenders could lose their jobs or be convicted of crimes they had never committed which, in turn, could result in imprisonment, torture, or worse. Hardly anyone dared stay away. On the other hand, the ever-growing masses in the streets made individual freedom of movement almost impossible. Thousands of people were searching for the exact place where they had been told they would find their assigned groups. And as the hours passed, the chaos only grew.

* * *

I got up that morning at six. I was supposed to meet my Béla Bartók School of Music colleagues at eight in one of the side streets, near Arena Alley. As the Party Secretary of our school had emphasized in previous meetings, our main task that morning was to locate our fellow students at the appropriate assembly place—pianists with pianists, singers with singers, percussionists with percussionists, string players with string players, and so on. Finding the right group, we had to form ever larger groups, which eventually would constitute the whole school. These orders sounded logical, even doable, but in the early morning, the throngs in the streets were so large that locating and uniting with our groups at first seemed impossible. Chaotic scenes ensued everywhere. Still, after many hours, despite the crowds and a number of failed attempts, we began to coalesce and find our proper places with our colleagues.

I was amazed by what I saw. Most of the youth groups of the Béla Bartók Musical Arts School and its Communist Party members carried Hungarian Republic flags and oversized slogans printed on posters. They also had victory banners and propaganda texts fastened on their fronts and backs, all celebrating the Hungarian Communist Party and its leader Mátyás Rákosi as well as the Soviet leadership. After standing and waiting again for several hours, we were encouraged to move on and parade past the huge platform at the edge of the trees in City Park, gesturing, singing, and shouting in unison our "eternal gratitude" to our leaders, the "great Stalin," the "wise Rákosi," and to other members of the Hungarian

Figure 1. Zsuzsi and Pista (1951–1952).

Communist Party who were standing on the platform. All of us knew that the Communist leadership was responsible for creating the humiliation, oppression, and exploitation practiced by the new system in Hungary and that this leadership was also responsible for the ongoing mass murder carried out by the Party and the government in dealing with the "enemies of the People's Republic," real or imagined. But most of us didn't dare talk about it or even to think about such discussions about these facts.

Marching in front of the tribunal, we were expected to demonstrate our "undying fidelity" to Stalin, to the "great Soviet leaders," and to Hungary's Communist leadership. And this we did. But it was not enough; we had to go on marching and screaming for another hour.

By three or four o'clock in the afternoon, we had apparently fulfilled our tasks for the day and were free to go home. In fact, we were "encouraged" to walk home, since the city's streetcars, buses, and taxis were insufficient to transport the huge masses of people.

As always on such occasions, I was filled with contempt and anger, disgusted and exasperated by the pressure under which we lived. After surviving the German occupation and the Holocaust, I thought that we would never again be exposed to such humiliation and such intimidation. How wrong I was! While this time we were not being attacked as Jews (those attacks would start in the early 1950s), we were being cheated and misled again and again; even worse, we were forced to live according to the lies of outrageous Soviet propaganda. Moreover, we were forbidden to discuss the current political situation with anybody who was not a "believer"—or even to question it. Hearing about the newly created internment camps such as Recsk and others in Hungary, we understood that all people there were taken without judicial sentence and tortured until they "confessed." I started to formulate for myself the facts of our lives: we live under a dictatorship. The promise my father made me during the Siege of Budapest in the basement of the White Cross Hospital, where we were hiding from both the Nazis and the falling bombs, that after liberation we would live as free people, never to be humiliated again, was untrue. We are now where we were then; this time, of course, not as Jews but as an entire nation. Over the years that followed, bitterly I repeated my father's "promise" to myself again and again.

The Soviet Union had been a partner of the Allies during the war; hence, the defeat of the Germans was not carried out by democratic and humanitarian states alone. In Hungary, we witnessed the "truth" of Communism—that is, the true face of totalitarian ideology became reality, a process and a result that also mirrored that of the Nazis. Following the directions of

Stalin, the Hungarian Communist government started to kill the general population—first, those among the intellectual leadership whom they saw as possibly threatening the system. Hence the menace of murder did not disappear, contrary to my father's promise in the bomb shelter during the Siege of Budapest. We were occupied by the Soviets and could do nothing about it.

2

Promise of the Night

Kati Fischmann lived in the northern part of Budapest, in Zugló, not too far from the edge of City Park. To get there I had to walk perhaps some twenty or twenty-five minutes, but I was happy to do so, happy to have the marches and the yelling behind me, and happy to think about the exciting adventure waiting for me. I had a red blouse on, a black skirt, wore new stockings, and my hair had been done by Erzsi the night before (Erzsi lived with us; she was my adopted sister, who had saved our lives during the Holocaust). With this preparation I felt secure to meet any boy in the world.

* * *

Figure 2. A group of forced laborers in the summer of 1944, among them my father. They are conscripted Jews, mostly from Budapest.

Kati was in the same class as my brother Iván in elementary school in Békéscsaba, the town in Hungary where our family lived from 1931 to 1941. This was where the Fischmanns, who were friends of my parents, lived as well. Tragically, however, the Fischmanns had stayed in Békéscsaba, where Kati's father was a radiologist, rather than move to Budapest as we had done in 1941. By sheer coincidence, because of our move we avoided deportation. I should have said by sheer luck! Jews in Budapest had not gone through the same treatment as Jews in the countryside had: most of them were not deported to Auschwitz while most Jews in the countryside were. Hungary's third anti-Jewish law (1941) had forced my father to sell his pharmacy (for half the price it was worth). Soon after, we moved to Budapest, where he started a new business with an old friend of his, Lajos Eisner, who was registered with the authorities as a "Decorated Jew" because of the Iron Cross he had received in the Hungarian army after World War I. This advantage meant that unlike the rest of the Hungarian Jews, who could no longer own their businesses, Mr. Eisner still could. My father invested the little money he received for his pharmacy into a bicycle shop, which was run under the name of Mr. Eisner, who did not "count" as a Jew. And since we lived in Budapest, we were not deported to Auschwitz during the summer of 1944, as was every other Jew in the countryside except a very few who escaped.

Deportations from Békéscsaba to Auschwitz started in June 1944. Our move from Békéscsaba took place three years before the German occupation of Hungary. But the Fischmanns did not leave. Medical doctors were allowed to see Jewish patients, and Dr. Fischmann continued his profession. After the Germans occupied Hungary in March 1944, however, the new laws forbade his work. And within two months of the country's occupation, deportations of those considered Jews began. Kati and her mother hid in somebody's house, but a couple of weeks later the two of them were denounced by one of their neighbors. Picked up by the Hungarian gendarmerie, they were forced into a boxcar and deported to Auschwitz. Mrs. Fischmann was murdered in the camp, but Kati, fifteen years old and strong, was lucky enough to stay alive and return home.

Meanwhile, her father and brother were drafted into the Jewish forced labor service. Both survived the war and the Holocaust. After liberation, the three Fischmanns moved back to Békéscsaba, where Kati finished high school. Ultimately, they moved to Budapest and Kati enrolled at the university, majoring in mathematics.

She visited us often. It was heartbreaking: her sense of time veered back and forth between past and present. She would still talk about her mother in the present tense as if she were still alive.

"Really? My mother also says that we must always do what we love," she would say, as if to remind herself, "and I think and believe this, just as my mother would." On the other hand, she did not hide the fact that she was lonely and preoccupied with Auschwitz. Feeling uncertain, desperate, and alienated, she would sometimes cry, "I don't know what to do or whom to turn to!" Once she asked me, "Do you think there is anybody I could talk to? All I see before me is the camp." I could not say that she should talk to me about it; I was frightened and shook whenever I heard details about Auschwitz. She appeared to me to be a helpless little girl, a lost orphan, and I was afraid that I might become one, too.

After the war, our fathers continued their friendship, so we remained close to one another. When the Fischmanns moved to Budapest, Kati started to visit us regularly. She was one of the first people who spoke to me about Auschwitz. Living with its memory, she told me about the horrors of this place: about Mengele, the gas chambers, hunger, her mother, and the dehumanization of the Jews. Also, she told me that sometimes in her dreams she would see her mother, who would turn into my mother after a while (the two women were friends in Békéscsaba). Once she told me, weeping, that hearing my mother speak, she would suddenly hear the voice of her mother. Obviously she was desperate about her loss and was feeling lonely, missing her mother's warmth and loving kindness. We invited Kati over often, but this, of course, could not assuage her pain or dim her memories. She could never forget the wounds inflicted upon her. But despite everything, she went to university and studied to become a mathematical physicist. Years later she married, had two children, and lived a happy and fulfilled life. The family moved first to Israel and later to the United States.

3

Encountering Pista

On the way to Kati's I left large throngs of people in City Park and its surroundings. I could not wait to reach her apartment. As I walked along, I thought of the young men she had invited for the evening. My heart was pounding: it was going to be a tremendously exciting adventure. I was looking forward to meeting them.

As I mentioned before, I did not know many young men. In Budapest I had met none of my brother's classmates; in the countryside most of the boys I knew had died in the Holocaust. Many had been killed in Budapest, too. In fact, during the siege of the city 160,000 people had perished. After the war, hunger and infectious diseases took the lives of a large number of young people, among them many children. In addition, some young Jewish

Figure 3. Erzsi (Erzsebet Fajo).

boys whose parents were friends of my parents had left Hungary and moved to countries where they were allowed to settle, while others had moved to what was then called Palestine. A few, however, were caught at the border and taken by the Russians to the Soviet Union. Most of these young men had never returned.

Walking to Kati's party, I thought again and again of the young mathematicians I was soon to meet, thinking they would probably be different from the musicians I knew: less audience-oriented and less self-conscious. Most of the young people I met at the Béla Bartók School of Music and the Ferenc Liszt Academy were preoccupied with their own artistic development—as was I, I must admit, with my own career.

But the young mathematicians whom Kati had invited were not just students in the math department at Budapest University; they were also members of Eötvös József College, Budapest, something that greatly impressed me. I had heard from my father that the students at Eötvös College were different from ordinary university students. An elite teacher training and scientific institution created in Budapest at the beginning of the twentieth century in the spirit of the French École Normale Supérieure, Eötvös College prepared its students to become elite researchers, members of the Hungarian Academy of Sciences, university professors, heads of

Figure 4. Zsuzsi and Pista.

secondary schools, and high school teachers. Eötvös College's admissions process was rigorous: only fifteen young men were accepted from the whole country per year. And among these students were some of the future leaders of Hungarian science and culture. My father often talked to me admiringly about Eötvös College, praising its high mission but always regretful that it did not accept young girls as students.

* * *

Kati opened the door to me. Curly brown hair framed her heart-shaped face, and her blue-green eyes twinkled behind her glasses. She made everyone feel welcome with her sweet and happy smile. Obviously she, too, was looking forward to the evening. I entered the apartment. Three first-year and three second-year university students, each studying physics and mathematics, stood up to introduce themselves to me. I had never seen such an attractive group of young men. Among the first-year students were Tamás Lipták and Tamás Kővári, both of whom became mathematicians, leaving Hungary for England in 1956. The third first-year student was Frigyes Károlyházy—later professor of theoretical physics at Budapest University. In the second group were László Pál, a mathematician, and Imre Izsák, who became a scholar of geodesy and celestial mechanics at Harvard University in the early sixties (he died soon after at the age of thirty-five). Izsák left Hungary in 1956, as did István Ozsváth, the third member of this group, who became a professor of mathematics in Dallas at the Graduate Research Center of the Southwest in 1963.

I had a short chat with each of these young men, noting that while they were all very intelligent and interesting, one of the second-year students, István, was exceptionally nice; good-looking (*more than good looking: beautiful*, I thought); open; polite; modest; and in an unusual way, very witty. He had deep and large, warmly shining light-brown eyes; a high forehead; a very intelligent quadrangular face; a straight, well-formed, and large nose; and an unforgettably sweet smile. He joked about the enthusiastic crowds in the park during the demonstrations and about our political leaders' celebrating themselves and one another. Also, he made fun of himself and the rest of his colleagues watching the celebration. He spoke in short, well-formed sentences, all of them essential to the points he made. He was at once moving, funny, and very attractive.

We talked about other issues as well. It was obvious that Kati had told the young men that I was a musician because soon after we began discussing the events of the day, they asked me to play something on the piano. I sat down and played Beethoven's Sonata in E-flat major, op. 27. At the end of the first part I stopped, but the young men asked me to continue. When I had finished the piece and turned around in my chair, I saw only five young men: the witty one with the beautiful large brown eyes, high forehead, square face, and large and funny nose was missing.

"How do you like them?" Kati asked after I stood up and followed her to the kitchen.

"Very much," I said, "but the one I liked the most—I think Ozsváth was his name—isn't here anymore! Where is he?"

"Oh," she said, "Pista?" (A short name for István in Hungarian.) "Sorry, he had to leave. He had a date with his girlfriend at seven."

"Gosh," I thought, "what a pity!" Then I said, "He's the nicest guy I've ever met—so handsome, so funny, and so modest—and he smiled at me so unspeakably sweetly!"

Despite Pista's early departure, the rest of us stayed at Kati's until ten o'clock, when the young men accompanied me home. As I went to bed I could hardly think of anything else but Pista, the young man who had left so early, the one with whom I got to exchange just a few words. I had never in my life seen anyone so handsome, so attractive, and so strangely witty.

A few days later Kati called me to confess that she had talked to Pista about me and had told him that I liked him very much. I was angry when I heard this and felt betrayed, but Kati told me not to feel so, because Pista had told her that ever since he had met me and listened to the first part of that Beethoven sonata, he could think of nothing else. When I heard this, my heart was pounding. Then in addition to a deeply felt calm, an almost inconceivable happiness swept over me. A few hours later Kati called again to say that she and Pista had met at the university cafeteria, and he had mentioned that he would like to invite me to a big party planned by the students at Eötvös College. They were to perform a play they had written and had been enthusiastically rehearsing for the past several months. Before the dancing was to begin the night of the party, some of those involved in organizing and directing the play would also perform it.

Kati was excited by this news, as was everybody who heard about it. There was a reason for this, as I later found out. It was generally known by both students and faculty that this particular play would poke fun at Eötvös College itself as well as at the university, its students, professors, and the Communist leadership—a prospect which at this point in Hungarian political life was both exciting and unnerving. The students knew, as did everyone else, that the system would not tolerate any attempt to ridicule life in Hungary under the Communist Party. Kati told me that she was worried about the future of the college.

"Who knows what will happen after this performance... There is only one thing we know for sure," she added. "Only after the play will the dancing begin."

I could hardly believe that these plans were going forward. I tried to suppress the feeling of danger that "outsiders" seemed to be worried about and to think of nothing but the dream becoming true: meeting Pista again. The mere idea of being with him made me imagine that everything would be illuminated by moonlight, surrounded by rainbows, as in dreams or fairy tales, and a silver path would lead away from the cruel, cold, and dangerous world in which we lived. I felt as if some miraculous hand had opened up a world of beauty, color, and happiness, far removed from the never-ending fear and oppression with which we had to live first under German and later Russian occupation.

* * *

The day of the party arrived, and I set out for Eötvös College, which was quite far from our place. My father wanted to accompany me. He was worried about the play's starting as late as seven.

"That means," he said, "that dancing won't start until ten, so what time should I come to pick you up?"

"I'll call you," I assured him. "Or I'll take a taxi."

He took me there. But when the party was over, I didn't take a taxi. Pista brought me home at daybreak.

This was the first night Pista and I spent together. It opened up a new world to me, one in which life was beautiful, funny, strange, and filled with love. It was a life in which I was not afraid—at least as long as I was with him. There were no wars in that world, no fighting, no fear, no suffering, no humiliation: just happiness. But, of course, when I was not with him, I feared that I would lose him.

* * *

We sat through the play which, as István pointed out, was an accurate caricature of everyday life at Eötvös College under the Communist system, and he enjoyed it so much that he remembered its details to the end of his life, never forgetting the songs he learned that night. Significantly, these songs had the same effect on almost all students of Eötvös College present at this performance; when they met fifty years later, they would still sing them to one another. Indeed, by making fun of both the college and the Communist system, these songs showed how the Party's views were spread, concealing the past and blanketing everything with meaningless ideology. The authors of the play had spoofed themselves as well as the ruling political regime and its adherents, including Party members at the college, their political stance, confusing decisions, threats, and nonsensical claims, abusing the college's name and reputation to spread their version of "truth." The satire mocked the behavior of the Communist leaders and their eager followers as well as that of regular students and professors in the college and still others in "real life." Not yet knowing most of those who were lampooned in the play, I didn't quite understand it all; to do so took many years. But still I knew that the attack was astonishing, and I knew that I was witnessing a major moment in Hungarian cultural life. I also knew that by now the destruction of Eötvös College had been on its way for a long time.

After this performance Eötvös College functioned for a short while as if nothing had happened. One day, however, on orders from the Communist Party, the government forced the college to leave behind its eminent past, becoming like any other place housing university students. The play alone had not been the only cause of this decision. The prestigious past of the college didn't belong in the "new world." It had to cease

Figure 5. Pista's parents in the 1950s.

to be what it was; hence, it was degraded by the country's Communist leadership, who pushed to eliminate "elite" institutions in a move representative of "the new goals of the university," which were against any "difference." After a while the college was reconstituted, but it has never again become the same institute of the elite; rather, it was turned into one of the dormitories of Budapest University.

4

In the Garden

After the play the music started, and we began to dance. As soon as Pista took me in his arms, I felt that I had arrived in a place I would never have to leave as long as I lived. This was a new experience for me. Throughout my childhood, love for my parents was always connected with fear that I would lose them. I constantly feared that my father would be murdered by the Nazis and later by the Communists. And it took years for me to learn the circumstances under which my parents' brothers and sisters were killed during the Holocaust. The more I knew, the more frightened I became and this fear never left me. I had seen with my own eyes Hungarian National Socialists shooting Jews into the Danube and Russian soldiers shooting men and women alike in the streets. In addition, when the Communists came to power in Hungary (1947–56), we had known several families whose fathers, husbands, or sons had been taken away, tortured, and eventually murdered. Some of them, like Zoltán Horváth (a Social Democratic journalist), were tortured for many years and freed only in 1956. Our former neighbor Dr. László Benedek, arrested in 1951, met with the same fate. And after I learned about my Uncle Pali's murder on the Russian front in the winter of 1941–42 by members of the Hungarian army, I was afraid for my father every day as long as he lived. I had the same fears when I thought of my mother and brother, and sometimes my best friends.

The sense of security I felt in Pista's arms was new to me and unexpected. When he was near me, I was grateful to be alive. But these feelings lasted only as long as he was nearby; when he was not, I feared for his life just as I did for my father's. But living with him for decades after we came to the United States, I started to believe that we would stay together until we died.

* * *

We danced for a while and forgot the world, dizzy from seeing just each other. Then we left the dance floor and went outside to talk. Sitting on a bench in the silvery moonlight in the garden of Eötvös College, we talked about everything that was important in our lives. I spoke of my parents, about their suffering during and after the Holocaust when they finally came to understand that there was no hope of their brothers' and sisters' return. I also spoke about Erzsi, my adopted sister, who had saved us from death during the mass killings of the Jews in Budapest. Pista wept. I looked at him, stunned. I had never seen a man cry except for my father when he found out about his brother's death in Russia, and our friend Géza Varga, who had sobbed when talking about his eight-year-old daughter, Julika, being dragged with her mother into the gas chamber at Auschwitz.

Then Pista spoke. He told me of his deep gratitude to a Mr. Popper, who had a tiny grocery store in the town of Kölesd, the town where he grew up. Apparently, one day after Pista had completed fourth grade, Grandfather Ozsváth went to visit Mr. Popper in his shop. They talked for a little while, and then Mr. Popper asked his friend a question that had obviously been preoccupying the old man for quite a while.

"What will your Pista do next fall? Is he going to go to high school?"

At that time in Hungary, children could start high school (gymnasium) after four years of elementary school. It would take them eight more years to get a diploma, which would allow them to apply to a university. Or they could continue their studies by enrolling in the fifth and sixth grades of their elementary school which, however, would lead to no further level of education. This was also the case with a third type of schooling that offered four years after elementary school.

"No," said Pista's grandfather. "We can't afford it!" There was no high school in Kölesd. In fact the nearest was in Gyönk, a town about twenty miles away. "So," the grandfather continued, "the boy would have to live in a dormitory, coming home just once a week."

"Well," answered Mr. Popper—and Pista's voice broke here as he told me the story—"we've decided that our daughter Klára will go to high school no matter what—even if we have to eat potatoes for the next eight years."

"If the Poppers can afford it, so can we," said Pista's grandfather when he got home and took off his coat.

Repeating this statement more than a few times, the Ozsváths enrolled Pista in the gymnasium at Gyönk.

"That's why," he told me, "I am forever grateful to Mr. Popper. Without him I wouldn't have gone to the gymnasium. I could never have applied to and would never have been accepted at my university, never been a student at Eötvös College, and never become a mathematician!" He smiled, and happiness lit up his serious, sweet face. "And, of course, I would never have met you! That's why I'll never forget what this man did for me." Then, looking at me, his eyes shining with tears, he said, "And did you know that Mr. Popper was Jewish?"

"No," I said.

"Yes," he sighed, "that's the problem. I can't tell him how grateful I am! He was killed in Auschwitz, and so was his entire family except Klára, his grandchild and my classmate, who is still alive!"

We fell silent. All around us the spring perfume of flowers, grass, and trees wafted through the air. "Do you know about Auschwitz?" he asked me quietly, sighing into the darkening night.

"Yes, I do," I answered—and suddenly I heard the screaming voices of the guards, saw the change of the landscape to the crematoria, the gas chambers, the forced laborers, among them my uncles and aunts. Except for Erzsi, I had never had an exchange like this with any non-Jew in Hungary. This was definitely not a topic of discussion in 1949—not in the country whose gendarmerie had delivered half a million Jews to Auschwitz and whose military had killed fifty thousand Jewish slave laborers on the front, years before the Germans occupied the country. In addition, in 1944, twenty-two thousand Hungarian gendarmes carried out the deportation of half a million Jews. These facts were deeply suppressed by the population and the leadership alike. In fact, people were more inclined to refer to Hungary's own pain during the war: the number of people killed in Russia and those who died of infectious disease, hunger, bombs, German brutality, Russian brutality, and later the new persecutions by the Communist government. General indifference, including perhaps some never-formulated sense of guilt for Jewish losses—the death of half a million murdered Jews—was usually not a topic of discussion among non-Jews in Hungary for many years after the war, whether in Budapest or the countryside.

"And when I think," Pista said, "that my countrymen put these people into boxcars and delivered them to those murderous places, I am shaken by despair and a cold shiver runs down my back."

My mouth stood open. "Why do you say this? How do you know all this?" I asked.

"Well," he said, "first of all, every Jew disappeared from my village. And while I kept on asking about them, I got answers that made me recognize that I still don't really know anything. Then I had a teacher in Gyönk at the high school—Jenő Lengyel was his name. I think he was Jewish, although I am not sure. But it was he who told me about the tragic end of Jews in

Hungary. He talked to me about Auschwitz and taught me Latin as well. And in fact it was he who encouraged me to apply to Eötvös College and the university in Budapest."

Listening to Pista's words, I was amazed by the independence of his thinking. When I asked him about his childhood, he told me about Kölesd, the town he came from, and about his family—his sister, who was a very good student in high school; his mother, father, and grandparents, all of whom were simple farmers. But there was so much love in his description of their lives and the world in which they lived that I was extremely touched by the depth of his thoughts and understanding of his own roots, including his emotional-intellectual development.

Then he kissed me. It was the first kiss I had ever received from someone I found attractive, intelligent, and interesting. As we embraced each other on the bench, I was overwhelmed by a sense of immersion into that night, feeling the power of heavenly love in every bush and flower, coming from the moon and sky above. I was swooning. I wanted to stay longer, not wanting to get up from that bench or leave. We kissed and kissed. But slowly, the sky started to lighten, and morning would soon break through the darkness. I thought of my father, knowing that he would be worried. I knew I had to go home.

As we started to leave the garden, we could still see the crescent moon, but then the sky turned lighter and we began our long walk home.

* * *

It was daylight by the time we arrived at 10 Abonyi Street, the house where I lived with my parents, brother, and Erzsi. Pista and I said farewell to one another in the spring-green garden. I felt as if I were in a dream. I realized that I had met a young man whom I loved and trusted as much as I had ever loved and trusted anyone besides my parents. He was more attractive and good-looking than anyone I had known and, I thought, he was just like my parents and Erzsi: a person who would risk his life if needed to save others, my criterion for friendship and love in the world—a notion I first formulated during the Holocaust.

At home, I told my father all about Pista, and I thought about him day and night.

5

The First Visit

A week passed before I saw him again. From that day on we met every Sunday afternoon. During the week he was going to classes and studying, and so was I. But Sundays were ours. For most of the week he had to stay at the observatory, where he worked as a researcher. His observations of the stars could, of course, take place only at night. But after he passed his exams for the Candidate Degree (comparable to the post-proposal status of PhD students in the United States), the situation changed. By then, he had already done the work that involved observation of the stars. He did not need to spend most of his time at the observatory to complete his dissertation; rather, he had to calculate a large number of long equations and formulate his ideas. All of this he could do anywhere, so he was at home during the weekends and sometimes even during the week. But on Sundays, the two of us were still usually together.

His first visit to us came a week after the big party at Eötvös College. Over the years, my parents had known my previous "boyfriends" but, of course, they did not take them very seriously. Meeting Pista, however, was different. He was just twenty years old, yet he impressed them deeply. They found him respectful, humble, honest, witty, and brilliant, becoming involved with him in important discussions. At first they discussed his studies, the university, and the branch of mathematics he loved. But after a while, the three of them started to discuss the political developments at Eötvös College, the place's glorious past, its threatened present, and its inevitable future destruction.

After the first long talk with my parents, Pista turned to me and asked me to play the Beethoven sonata I had performed at Kati's a few weeks before. I started the piece from the beginning and played it to the end. He was enchanted. "I've never heard anything like that in my life! Would you please play it again?"

I did. Then, shaking his head in utter delight, he pulled out a pencil from his pocket, asked for a piece of paper, and sat down at the table so that there was place for both of us next to one another. He drew a triangle.

"Now," he said, "I'll show you something else that is breathtakingly beautiful . . ." He began to describe something "fabulous" and "delightful" about calculations related to the triangle—but unfortunately, I didn't understand it. I couldn't even pretend to follow his argument. Hence, I could not claim that he had successfully communicated to me the sublimity of his proposed solution of the problem. He drew the triangle again and again, trying to explain the same idea and the "extraordinary simplicity, clarity, and beauty of the solution." Yet I did not understand the claim then or even later. As a matter of fact, I failed to see the "breathtaking beauty" of almost all mathematical concepts he tried to tell me about during our life together. But my inability to understand them did not keep him from bringing up these concepts in an attempt to demonstrate the particular problems and solutions he was preoccupied with, and their inherent magnificence. Yet he was never impatient or disappointed when I failed to follow his ideas; rather, he would smile patiently and reassure me that next time I would get it. I never did, though, ashamed as I am to admit it.

After trying unsuccessfully for the first time to show me the beauty of this particular math proof, he put away paper and pencil, and we went out for a walk in the green, rose-scented neighborhood. I felt as always when I was with him, great pleasure, security, and fulfillment such as I had never felt with anyone else. The sky was bathed in a golden light, the flowers of the bushes were gleaming. I realized that ever since the Holocaust and the Siege of Budapest I had been living with fear, which affected my life from childhood to adulthood. With Pista around, however, I was no longer afraid but rather delighted and amused; I could even laugh about myself.

6

The Rise of Terror

When he came the next Sunday, we talked about his parents and his future. He explained to me the political pressure under which his family lived, the pressure which had begun to take on catastrophic dimensions by the middle of 1949. Until then, having spent almost no time in the countryside, I had no direct experience of the misery in which the peasants found themselves under Soviet rule in Hungary. While I had known about their general poverty throughout history, I did not know about the terrible demands forced upon them by the Communist state. Sure, I knew that for many centuries they had been required to pay dues to the landowners. I also knew that during the Turkish occupation in the sixteenth century, their status weakened even more as they were forced to pay taxes not only to the landlords but also to the Ottomans, the Hungarian state, and the Church. But then, I knew that by the 1830s the country's gradual political improvement had helped start the process of emancipation for large masses of peasants. And I knew that finally, their serfdom ended in 1867, when they became free. But I did not know that almost eight decades went by before they were completely emancipated from the demands of the landlords on whose land they lived. And while they had been freed from all pressures for a couple of years after World War II, the peasants were now being oppressed by the Communist state.

In addition, it was important to know that by the twentieth century, the groups of rich as well as moderately situated peasants had started to use capitalistic production, methods which worked for profit. Still, the problem of their status was not completely resolved: only 40 percent of them belonged to the first group; 60 percent either had no land or, if they did, their plots were too small to provide an acceptable standard of living.

As a result, the so-called "landless peasants" still had to work more for their landlords than for themselves. They often led miserable lives: hungry and desperate, they were left to their own devices, many of them living at a barely human level. They as well as those who spoke for them believed that their misery would end if they were given enough land to support themselves. It appeared as if this time had arrived after World War II, when the newly created Hungarian state took away the land from the large estate owners and distributed it among the landless peasants. "The rich were chased away, but the poor got their share," was the way those who believed in true "liberation" characterized the issue. By 1948 to 1950, however, the Hungarian state, following the lead of Stalin's peasant policies, decided to nationalize every spot of land. This decision shook the peasants to the core. After centuries of fighting, they had lost again: not only would they be denied more land, but they would lose what they had received at the end of the war.

Over fifty years, Pista's parents and grandparents had been in the process of becoming increasingly independent. His great-grandparents—originally liberated serfs on an estate near the town of Kölesd—set aside every penny to buy land and become "landlords" as fast as they could. Still, it took much time and the help of their children, even grandchildren, before they scraped together about thirty or forty acres of wheat-producing land during the first few years of the twentieth century. At this point they started to look forward to the arrival of a better future when they could buy more land and become "well-to-do." But then in 1914, World War I broke out, lasting till 1918. During this time Hungary lost 383,000 young man on the front. In addition, hundreds of thousands of people died of various illnesses, cruel poverty, and starvation after the war.

As a young man, Pista's father was drafted to fight on the front. After a year, however, he fell into the hands of the French army and became a prisoner of war. Spending almost two years in France while his parents tried their best to work and survive without their son, he returned in 1919—a year after the war was over. At this point most Hungarians were living under difficult circumstances. The Trianon Peace Treaty had eliminated much of historical Hungary: as a matter of fact, the country lost two-thirds of its size and one-third of its population. More than three million Hungarians belonged now to newly created states and newly established borders. Still, peasants with some land lived better than before. By working hard during the late twenties and early thirties, Pista's parents saved enough money to buy another ten to fifteen acres of land as well as a small vineyard.

After terrible losses, general despair, and the crises of World War I, in addition to the rise of a cruel Communist government in 1919 and the Depression of 1929, Hungarians hoped to recover. But bitter nationalism spread along the thousand-year-old country when its large territories were cut away by the Allies, who wished to resolve the constant uprisings of the large number of nationalities living in Hungary. At this point many people were ready for the extreme political changes the Right proposed, especially during the Depression. Promising the resurrection of a greater Hungary, Hitler felt satisfied with the new Hungarian nationalist movement. In the late 1930s and early 1940s, he "gave back" some of the land taken from Hungary in 1919. But he swept the country into a new war. Yet again the outcome was disastrous: Hungary lost three hundred thousand soldiers and more than six hundred thousand civilians—among them five hundred thousand Jews and twenty-eight thousand Roma.

Change came slowly. Still, after the end of World War II, in which roughly a million people died, Hungarian peasants started life again.

* * *

Like almost every peasant who lived through these difficult times, Pista's parents and grandparents worked hard to produce food, doing their best to improve their own lives and those of the people in the town of Kölesd. The Communist government under Stalin, however, which took power after 1947, disapproved of a productive, self-sufficient peasantry. Following the Soviet model of forced collectivization, it attempted to repeat the actions of Stalin's policies during the 1930s, when five to ten million peasants, even those who had no more than thirty or thirty-five acres, were deported to Siberia. Most of these people froze to death or were worked to death. Those who remained in the villages, including their wives and children, were compelled to work the land. But most Russian peasants did not want to comply with the orders of the Communist Party. Nor did they want to give up the land they had wanted to own for centuries—the very land they felt belonged to them. Their will was broken, however. With torture and murder, Stalin's forces wiped out most people in these groups: those who resisted and those who didn't.

Fifteen to twenty years on, their Hungarian counterparts had the same reactions, the same emotions, and the same hope. They were unwilling to give away the land they thought they owned, the land on which their ancestors and they themselves had worked their whole lives. After World War II, when they finally received their portion from the state, they could not imagine that anyone would want to take away what they had suffered for through the centuries. They could not believe that this was a possibility.

They did not know what had happened in Russia during the 1930s. Hence by 1950, following the political developments in the Soviet Union, the Hungarian Communist Party began to arrest and incarcerate peasants who had more than thirty or thirty-five acres of land. In fact, the Party turned against them with the same fury that the Soviet leadership had turned against the Russian peasants twenty years before. And just like their Russian counterparts, the Hungarian Communist leadership was ready to have them killed. Labeling the "rich" peasants as "enemies of the people," the Hungarian government called them *kulaks*, persecuting and punishing them, even if these owned no more than a few acres of land.

The conflict was deepening. Obviously, many peasants were unwilling to give up the land for which their ancestors had suffered for centuries: they wanted to own it, no matter how small the piece in their possession—a vain wish indeed. Like the Soviet leaders, the Hungarian Communist government tolerated no such resistance. Not content with punishing the resisting peasants, it imprisoned even those who did not protest. That is what happened in Kölesd, Pista's hometown. His father was one of the many peasants who had been arrested. Defined as a kulak, he spent almost two years in prison, working on the fields for the state.

This happened later, however—during the period from 1951 to 1953, a year after my first discussions with Pista about his life and background. In 1949 and 1950, the terror had not yet reached its peak in the countryside, but the war against the peasants was already underway. Recognizing the chain of events in Russia, Pista could foresee the threat to his parents and talked about it with great concern.

He also spoke about his little sister Marika, two years younger, to whom he was very close and whose illness worried him deeply. Her heart was dangerously large and her heartbeat almost twice as fast as it should be, he said. Her illness had been aggravated in childhood by a recurrent strep throat—untreatable in the 1930s and early 1940th since there was no penicillin and no help for tonsillitis. As a result, she became ill again and again. After a while, she developed rheumatic fever that affected her heart.

"If you look at her, you can see her fast heartbeat on her neck. It is quite visible," he told me sadly.

While worried about her health, István was very proud of her exceptional intelligence, as was she of his. One of the best students in high school, she followed in her brother's footsteps by enrolling in the gymnasium and after graduation applying to the University of Budapest, where she was accepted into the mathematics department. As he talked to me about her, his pride, his fear, his concern, and his love for her were written on his face.

* * *

The relationship between the two of us continued to intensify over the coming months. István visited me every Sunday, and we often stayed at home. We had great conversations about God, books, the Jews, and religion in general as well as our past, the oppression under which we lived, our future, and our hopes. I would play for him the piano pieces I was studying, he would show me his "beautiful mathematical proofs," and we would read our favorite poems to one another. I was touched to the core by his love of poetry: his sense of beauty; his musical perception of the lines and words; his love of the poem as song; his understanding of its rhythm, structure, and beat; its allegorical underpinnings, metaphorical expressions—all this amazed me. I did not expect such insight and sensitivity from someone not directly involved in the realm of the humanities. I have never tried to formulate all of this before, but as we read and recited hundreds of poems to one another—some already known, some we read for the first time—I saw again and again how deeply he identified with them, how much they meant to him, and how delighted he was when we read them together.

We often went to the mountains in Buda, where we would lie down on a blanket on the grass in the forest and exchange passionate kisses. Looking up, we could see the trees and birds, with the blue sky periodically peeking through. We completely forgot everything else in the world, consumed with love for one another. But we did not forget poetry: we would recite in whispers some of the most beautiful lyrics of Hungarian and German literature, reciting the poems of Petőfi, Arany, Ady, Radnóti, Attila József, Goethe, Schiller, and others. I had learned German as a child at home, and he had learned it in the gymnasium in Gyönk. He sometimes also recited Dante, whom he loved, having studied Italian language and poetry in high school for several years.

* * *

I always felt secure in his arms, as secure as on the day he first embraced me. I also knew from the beginning that we would be together for the rest of our lives. I knew that I could rely on him, that my world would be safe with him, and that in this deep love for one another, we had found our paradise: the sun, the trees, the flowers of May, the colors of the afternoon and the night, the bright shade and light of the world.

Of course, I had close friends as well, and living through the Holocaust and the Siege of Budapest, I knew what true friendship meant. Many of them had lost their families during the Holocaust but, like me, all of them spoke about the importance of being prepared to save others. This idea preoccupied me, as I had never forgotten our own time of persecution. It had been a major factor in my life, a criterion for ordering my world, my connections with others, and my friendships. My relationship with Pista shared this aspect as well: I knew that if friends of ours were ever persecuted, he would save them just as I would.

But there was something more between us too: I felt at home when I was with him. Loving my father and mother and constantly worrying about them, I was often overwhelmed by panic when they weren't around me. This fear went back to my early childhood, when I was afraid that I might lose them because the Germans would kill them. And after the war, as soon as I became aware of the new world of atrocities committed in the name of Communist ideology, this fear only intensified. At this point, I was afraid of the new government, the Russians, the Communist leadership, and the Hungarian police, the forces which were once again arresting and executing people in the country—I could not talk about it with almost anybody. If I mentioned my concerns to my parents, they would worry about me and try to calm me down as much as they could. They acted as if the past could not be repeated, claiming that what was happening now was the result of competition among the great powers rather than a new terror, which in their opinion was largely exaggerated by those who believed the Rightist propaganda. Anxious about me, they were unwilling to discuss the oppression under which we lived. Their friends had similar reactions; they pretended not to know what I was talking about. My close friends knew the nature of my concerns, however, and felt the same way, so we tried to separate ourselves from the world of our parents' generation, who were dealing with us as if we were children, acting as if we were blind and immature.

Remembering the past, Pista, my friends, and I recognized the threats of both the present and future; thus, we never stopped worrying about our loved ones. After a while, however, we found a solution: we became preoccupied with our early memories, recalling our childhood, inventing games, and imagining ourselves as major characters of the fairy tales we knew or of stories we made up ourselves. We decided that rather than live in the real world, we would spend time in the realm of legend and fantasy, holding fast to our childhood. Role-playing allowed us to maintain our image of real life as cruel, cold, and undesirable, while our games gave us a sense of enjoyment—at times, even hope for survival. Fantasy games like the ones I had played with my friends during the German occupation became our favorite means of communication from the end of the 1940s until we left Budapest in 1957.

It was when I met Pista that we started to play these games again. With him around I felt I could easily enter the magical place that allowed me to turn my back on the world of fear and menace; I could feel in me the power of love for this young man. In this new beautiful world, I felt able to escape the cruelty of the real one, at least as long as we were together. Understanding both the beauty and cruelty that surrounded us, I also was deeply aware of the change that Pista's presence created in me. The perception that our story was both real yet magical gave me a sense of happiness and great security. We lived with this realization every minute of every day, and this feeling never left us. It characterized our relationship for the entirety of our lives.

7

Fear

As under any dictatorship, the ideological pressure on the Hungarian population created a constant dialogue among close friends and a complete silence among others. People were frightened of one another. To me it was quite alarming that the world essentially remained unchanged after the Russians "liberated" us. Legal procedures were disregarded and human rights were trampled on.

When the war ended I still believed what my father had repeatedly told me over the years: after the Germans were defeated, a moral world would replace the one built on injustice and murder. Shortly after the war my parents found out that besides their brothers and sisters, most of their friends had been killed in the Holocaust. Some people, among those who survived, became ardent supporters of the Soviet Communist system, which spread rapidly in Hungary. Yet despite their passionate belief in the system, more and more people were arrested toward the end of the 1940s. And I heard frightening tales about the prisons to which they were taken. Indeed, at this point, prisons and concentration camps were created in Hungary as well as all over Eastern Europe. We learned that in these places, torture and executions were used to eliminate those who were declared to be "enemies of the people," and that such declarations were completely arbitrary. We knew about people who had belonged to the Social Democratic Party before, during, and after World War II—people who felt that their major political goal was to establish a socialist Hungary while resisting both the Hungarian fascist leadership and the Communist takeover. These people were persecuted not only in the semi-fascist Horthy era but also in "liberated" Hungary. In fact they were the first ones to be persecuted from 1947 to 1949. Secret as well as public trials were held, and the accused were tried, tortured, and eventually executed.

After a while, we heard heartbreaking news about the murder of Jewish groups. Some Soviet Jewish writers were arrested in Russia. They became defendants in the JAC (Jewish Anti-Fascist Association) trial. Later, I heard again that a large number of the Jews connected with this trial had been arrested and killed between 1948 and 1953, accused of being "Zionist traitors." The persecution, show trials, and murder of Jews had indeed restarted now in Russia. In fact, most critics of Soviet Communism emphasize that only Stalin's sudden death in March 1953 put an end to the antisemitic atrocities and a possible mass murder of Jews in the Soviet Union. Still, in addition, we heard about other major arrests, show trials, and camps set up to punish the accused—in Russia as well as in Hungary and in other "peoples' democracies"—many of whom were killed or convicted and forced to live under the harshest conditions for years.

The world in which we lived dashed all earlier humanitarian hopes for a better place: it was clear that despite World War II and the defeat of Nazi Germany, an all-powerful dictatorship was again not only possible but even functional. I felt secure only when we were all at home or when I was in Pista's arms, when I practiced the piano, when I played games with my closest friends, or when I listened to music, read, and recited poetry. After a while, I started to see that Pista was as victimized by the system and as vulnerable as anyone else. In fact, my feeling about his stability changed. I discovered that he was directly threatened as the son of kulaks, and I trembled at the thought that something might happen to him.

Was I right? How did he react to the rising, cruel dictatorship? First of all, with humor. He made fun of the ongoing rage; thereby, he was certainly less frightened than me. Making fun of the brutal ideology, he pointed out its absurdity and illogical findings. Also, he would declare over and over that we loved one another, that this love was strong enough to help us live untouched even during the cruelest political circumstances, and that we would therefore be able to survive and keep ourselves free from the threats and murderous practices of the state and the brutal power of Soviet politics. That is, he simply believed that having each other, we could live happily ever after, whether the Communists or others were ruling this earth. And then, just looking into his warm, smiling, intelligent, handsome face; into his light-brown, loving eyes and imagining myself forever in his arms, I forgot about my fears. As a matter of fact, sometimes I even felt strong enough to convince myself that indeed we could never be separated.

During the show trials, however, resounding all day and all night on the radio, the political atmosphere turned even more hostile in Hungary. I became ever more aware of the world of terror and started to grow ever more concerned about our future.

8

Hunger

The serum laboratory, which my father finally did successfully establish after our return to Békéscsaba in 1945, had been nationalized in 1948, as was my father's pharmacy, which he had had to sell for half its value in 1941. In 1944 all property was taken away from the Jews—without compensation. Change came after the war in 1945 when the Jews, if they were still alive, got back their businesses. At this point, my father got back the pharmacy. Unfortunately, however, his attempts to run a new serum lab kept him from paying much attention to the pharmacy. He employed a pharmacist whose task was to take over the business so that my father could spend time building up his serum lab. But the new pharmacist spent almost all the money the pharmacy earned for his own purposes. Then in 1949, when all private businesses in Hungary were nationalized, my father lost ownership of both his lab and his pharmacy. We were deeply grateful that he was able to find a job in Budapest as a chemist-pharmacist of the country's largest serum-producing firm, Phylaxia.

Yet despite the government's nationalizing both of his businesses the same year, the court held my father responsible for the debts the substitute pharmacist had run up in Békéscsaba. As the owner, my father was responsible for them. This meant that more than half his monthly salary from Phylaxia was deducted for many years to come. The court decision was handed down in 1949. The high cost of food and clothing caused misery for everybody in Hungary during this time period. But with his salary cut by half, my father brought home barely enough money to feed two people. And there were four of us. That meant we were hungry again, almost as hungry as during the Siege of Budapest. We could certainly not buy anything we would enjoy; in fact, to eat a slice of *dobos torta* (chocolate cake with a caramel cover) once or twice a month, I would have to walk home from Pest to Buda (a ninety minute walk) and back in freezing weather, snow, rain, or the heat of summer. If I did not eat a slice of dobos torta, I had money for my bus or streetcar fare. Sometimes I chose the cake; others I chose the bus. Each time I regretted my choice.

Thinking back, I now realize that Pista probably had even less to eat than my parents and me. At our house, we had at least some bread and pig fat, which my father brought home from the serum lab. Each week he was given a large piece of raw bacon, which my mother melted down into fat, then froze. We ate it day and night as a spread on bread, or my mother used it to fry some meager rations. The fat came from pigs whose blood was used to manufacture serum. It was also a way the plant justified the low salaries of its employees, claiming that it provided food for them as well as money. Just as during the Siege of Budapest, when we sat in the cellar hiding from the bombs, we talked again about food we would love to eat but could only imagine in our fantasy: chocolate cookies, cherry strudel, strawberry cake—and we were so hungry!

Until the fall of 1949, Pista received two packages a month from home. Each contained chunks of homemade bacon and a whole ring of homemade sausage. But by the winter of 1950 the packages stopped coming, as there was nothing more in Kölesd to send to Pista. The Ozsváths had to return nearly all the food they produced to the state: flour, wine, meat—all the meat of the pigs and calves they slaughtered. Everything. Pista's father had no more bacon or sausage to send to his son, who lived now on the bacon fat my father brought home from Phylaxia. We were all hungry; sometimes Pista was desperate. I will never forget one day when, just by chance, I met him in the street leading directly to the house where we lived. I had just left, while he was on his way home. I saw him from afar and ran into his arms.

"How are you, sweetheart?" I asked, happy to see him so unexpectedly.

His desperate answer was a blow to my heart: "I'm so hungry, so hungry, so hungry! Is there any food at home?"

"Just a piece of bread and some bacon fat," I said. I remember he almost cried: he had had the same for breakfast, the same for lunch the previous day, and the same for all his meals most of the time. His salary even when added to my father's was not enough to provide food for the four of us. Iván, my brother, was a medical student from 1947 to 1953. He often worked all night and sometimes went out on dates, sleeping at home just once or twice a week. He made some money and ate wherever and whatever he could. He was mostly independent from my father and no longer on his budget. But we were—Pista and I—and the money Pista made was barely enough to buy food for himself, and I earned no real money except what I received from my three piano students. We were starving! When Pista was at home with us, he ate what we did—a piece of bread with pork fat. But when he was not at home, he was tormented by hunger.

Also, he worried about his parents and had every reason to do so: the media attacked the peasants more and more aggressively, and arrests in the villages multiplied.

* * *

In the spring of 1950 the pressure on the peasants to turn back the land to the Communist state intensified. What the state wanted back was not only the land the peasants had received in 1945 during the official land distribution; it also wanted small plots of land these people had bought for themselves over the past few decades with their own savings. This was clear to every peasant concerned about the new war launched against them. Describing this war as "representing the common good," the Communist government did not hide its intentions, which aimed at state ownership of all the land in the country. Pista's concerns about his parents grew. Visiting them in Kölesd in the spring of 1951, he was still astonished by what his grandfather said:

"We can't understand why they haven't arrested your father by now! Every decent man of Kölesd is in jail! Why did they miss him?"

Six months later, Pista's father was arrested, too. At this point, Pista could not believe it, but there was nothing he or anybody else could do.

Mr. Ozsváth was sorely missed at home, not only as a husband and as a son but also as a worker on their farm. If Pista had not gone to Kölesd several times a year to help, they could never have managed the work by themselves.

9

The Wedding

One day in the spring of 1950, a friend of mine in the Béla Bartók School of Music asked me whether I thought my relationship with István would change if we were to be forced apart.

"What?" My heart was pounding. "Forced apart? Why would we be forced apart?"

"Oh!" she answered. "Haven't you heard?"

"What?" I asked, frightened.

"Oh," she went on, "everyone's talking about it. There can be no doubt that very soon Hungary, like other Eastern-European countries, will become part of Russia. Will be declared one of the states of the Soviet Union like Latvia, Lithuania, and Estonia were in 1940—when the populations were exchanged. Tens of thousands of people were arrested, deported, and resettled in the Soviet Union."

"The West wouldn't allow this," I replied, while I shook with fear.

"Well," she said, "as the West did nothing back then for them, it won't do anything now to save us! But," she said, "don't be afraid: they won't separate families."

Terrified, I went home. I called Pista at the observatory and asked him to come around for supper as soon as he could.

"Well," he said, "tonight is very difficult for me: I need to work on my dissertation. Could I come tomorrow? By that time, I will have finished some important calculations!"

"No!" I answered in panic. "Please come today. We're in great trouble. And please don't ask me why. Just come at six, before my father gets home."

He was great! He did not ask why. I sounded so frightened, he told me later, that he knew something had happened more significant than the trivial concerns of the day. And he knew, of course, that telephone calls on political issues were being recorded by government agencies whose task was to listen in on private conversations all the time.

He arrived at five o'clock.

"What's happened?" he asked, obviously quite worried.

We went for a walk. I told him the news. He had heard before, as I had now, about the threat of Hungary's being incorporated into the Soviet Union. But he never elaborated on these rumors, he told me, or on their possible consequences. Nor did he discuss them with anybody else, including me. He had suppressed them.

"I always do that with bad news," he admitted with a grin, which characterized his reaction to bad news for a lifetime. "That is, when the news is bad, I try to forget it!" Then he attempted to justify his approach: "I have to forget bad news, because I can't handle it," adding, "I couldn't do any work if I didn't do that."

"But this is different," I cried. "They will separate us!"

"And what can we do?" he asked. Seeing my sobbing, he became serious.

"Just one thing," I answered, thinking about the only solution that had occurred to me that morning. "If we get married, they won't tear us apart! The rumor is that they won't separate families from one another; they didn't do it in Lithuania or in Latvia."

"Really?" he smiled. Then he opened his arms to me, adding delightedly, "That's fabulous! We do have a solution then. Let's get married!"

We went home and agreed that I would talk to my parents that night, and only after that would he speak with them.

Before he left, he kissed me and held me tight in front of my parents, a display we had never performed in front of them before. Then, they went away.

"You're so tense tonight," my father said. "Is everything okay?"

"No, it isn't," I said desperately.

With a white face, he turned to me and asked, "What's wrong?"

I started to cry. "Rumor says that Hungary will go through the same process the Baltic countries had to go through. We'll be annexed to the Soviet Union. Haven't you heard it yet?"

"Yes," he said, "I have. But that doesn't necessarily mean that it will actually take place, nor that it will be the end of the world. As long as they let us stay together—and, of course, they would allow that—everything will be okay!"

Poor father! Having gone through the Holocaust and its aftermath, he had only one criterion for survival: whether or not we would be allowed to stay together as a family.

"Yes," I sobbed, "For us, because we are one family. But what about István? He doesn't belong to our family! They will separate us."

My parents were silent. They didn't know what to say.

"We have to survive even that kind of attack," said my father. "What else can we do?"

"There is one thing we could do," I said, panic-stricken. "We could get married and then, we wouldn't be separated."

My parents stared at me in complete despair.

"But you are only eighteen years old," said my mother, "and we don't live in the nineteenth century, when people married off their children at the age of sixteen."

"But we live in the twentieth," I sobbed. "This is a time when lovers can easily be separated because of the brutal treatment inflicted on us by the leading powers!"

"Okay," my father said. "Don't cry, my beautiful! We'll talk about this tomorrow. Perhaps you're right; perhaps the two of you should get married . . ."

Before I went to sleep, I called Pista at the observatory. "I believe they're going to allow us to get married," I whispered.

"Oh, my goodness!" Pista took a deep breath. "I'll visit you tomorrow."

He did visit and, going over the importance and absolute urgency of our marriage with my parents, he was happy and satisfied when they said yes.

Political pressure in Hungary intensified in the spring of 1950 as we prepared for our wedding, yet we were happy despite the misery and fear around us, despite the humiliation and horrifying laws of the system that kept its eyes open to monitor our actions, our decisions, and our future.

We got married on the first of June in 1950. It was a powerful event and I understood all its implications. I felt intensely that Pista and I were bound to one another forever, in life and in death, and that no human being and no human event could ever separate us.

10

Shadows and Light

In our great happiness and feverish preparations for the wedding, we also made a mistake, one which has haunted me all my life. Even today as I write these lines, I regret that we did not invite Pista's parents to the wedding. Why did we not invite them? It was because Pista said he did not want to be subjected to tense, lengthy, and unpleasant arguments with his family.

As soon as my parents agreed, I suggested, "Let's write to your parents," to which he replied in a quiet but resolute voice:

"No! For the time being, I'm not going to talk about this in Kölesd."

"Why?" I asked, bewildered.

"Because I don't want to argue," he said. Indeed, Pista's entire life may be characterized by the fact that he would never argue. He never created or participated in any conflict or controversial issue. He never wanted to win an argument or prove to others that his beliefs were truer than theirs (except in mathematics, of course, when he would argue passionately), nor did he ever have the urge to demonstrate that he was right.

It is hard to know what was the origin of this deep distaste for and terrifying angst of conflict with people, including his own family. Maybe he was born that way. Maybe his sweet, peaceful nature could not deal with any aggressive opposition. But it is also possible that this grew out of tension in the relationship between his grandmother and mother, a tension about which he often spoke to me, which overshadowed the Ozsváth family's happiness in Kölesd and never ceased to cause him pain in his lifetime. The truth of the matter is that he often witnessed major quarrels between his mother and grandmother. This was heartrending and frightening to him as a child because he loved them both, and the pain of their cruelty to each other hurt him. He told me that he felt trapped in their conflict and tried to avoid the feelings it aroused by refusing to listen to its details. He would simply leave the house and go to play with other children when his mother and grandmother were arguing and insulting one another.

I thought religious pressure was one of the major reasons for the tension between the two women. Pista's mother and her family came from a Lutheran background, while the ancestry of Pista's father was Calvinist. Such differences were not easily overcome during the 1920s, especially by the peasants, their pastors, and the churches in small Hungarian towns. In the end, Pista's mother had been forced to convert and regretted the consequences of her actions, as she told Pista, for the rest of her life.

Of course, there were some other "natural" tensions as well, connected to their ways of living, which magnified the conflict between the two women. The Ozsváth family shared one house, as did most families in the Hungarian countryside. It was a way of living that must have led to strained relationships among family members, especially those coming from different households, religions, and generations. Obviously, this made life for Pista's mother extremely difficult. Indeed, there were often scenes and disputes with her parents-in-law which, as Pista said, were never resolved. It is, of course, not easy to live in one house with other people among whom disputes and hostilities flare up quickly, especially for children. I noticed early in our relationship that Pista was sensitive to tension and disliked disputes more than anybody among my friends and my family. I believe that such disputes produced great fear in him when he was a child and that this feeling persisted throughout his lifetime. I believe that perhaps the war between his parents and grandparents must be one of the explanations for his deep desire for peace within the family and his virtual horror in the face of argument and altercation.

Still, it was his task and duty to tell his family about our marriage. But he simply said that he could not and did not want to tell them. In fact, he even pointed to some suicides in the family, believing they originated in family conflicts between wives and mothers-in-law. He also pointed out his parents' obvious objection to our plans and said they would try to influence my parents negatively, too. Clearly we were too young for marriage. In addition, I had not yet earned any money, and Pista had not finished the university studies for which his family had made immense financial sacrifices. Although he went home every summer for two or three weeks to participate in the harvest and spent several days in Kölesd every three or four months to help his parents with hard physical work, neither they nor he knew with certainty how long he would be able to do so. What would happen when he had a job? How would he be able to return to his town again and again? He told me that his parents had kept on paying tuition for him after he left Kölesd in 1939, spending a significant amount for his studies in the gymnasium, in addition to sending him biweekly food packages. They knew that he was to stay for almost four years at the university, and that during that time he hoped to fulfill his life's ambition to become a mathematician. Naturally, he said, they would also be worried that an early marriage would threaten this dream.

As for the future, they would be afraid that Pista might not want to go as often to Kölesd as he had. After he married and settled down somewhere, he might not want to perform the hard, physical work the yearly harvest demanded. In addition, he argued there were other reasons for treating this topic of discussion carefully; therefore, at least for the time being, he did not want to say a word about his plans. He claimed that they would ask questions he would not want to answer, such as "Is there perhaps a baby on the way?" or "How will you earn money for two people?" (a task which was almost impossible for a couple in Hungary during the early 1950s). And then the obvious question will be asked: "How will you support your family?" followed by the most important one: "How will you get an apartment?"—another almost impossible task in Budapest at this time.

"No," he told me, "I don't want to answer such questions, nor do I need to listen to my parents, warning me about getting married. In fact, I want to avoid screaming, yelling, emotional turbulence, and terrible scenes. I'll tell my family after the wedding that we got married, period." He repeated this statement often. It was impossible to change his mind even for my parents, who tried their best to convince him otherwise. So we kept our marriage secret.

* * *

Ten days after our wedding we took a train to Kölesd. Arriving home, Pista told his parents the news. At first they did not quite understand what had happened, or did they not want to understand? But when they processed what they had heard, my mother-in-law started to cry, and Pista's father and grandparents looked deeply disturbed. After a while, recovering from the first shock, they started to ask questions about the future, emphasizing that Pista's salary was barely enough to support one person; it could not support both of us, let alone a family. Pista's father also went on to describe their own financial situation, which left them with practically no money, food, wheat, grain, or wine—because they were obliged to deliver everything to the state. They repeated again and again that to marry under such circumstances was irresponsible because providing for a family had become impossible these days. There was only one argument they could not reason against and that was stated by Pista. He explained that we had to get married because this was the only way to prevent our separation; that is, marriage was the only means by which we could stay together. As they themselves were afraid of more restrictions and even of deportation, Pista's parents slowly came to understand the importance and even the urgency of our marriage. And after a few hours of excited disputation they seemed to forgive both of us for keeping our wedding secret. Finally, we embraced each other. Is it possible that they forgave us? I was never sure. But three days later we left Kölesd peacefully.

Over the years, our relationship with Pista's parents grew ever more loving. We visited them three or four times a year, and Pista always spent an extra two or three weeks in Kölesd to help during the summer. As the years passed, and we left Hungary, my in-laws and my parents became close friends, my father visiting them and overseeing their state of health for as long as he lived, a task which my brother Iván took over after my father's death. In fact, Iván took care of them until the end of their lives. And Pista's parents' affectionate, amazingly loving response has remained with us through all the years and will stay with me for as long as I live. I will never forget that in 1965, when I stood in front of my in-laws after eight years of separation, meeting them and my own family in Vienna, I held our ten-month-old baby Kathleen in my arms.

My mother-in-law kissed me, then kissed Kathleen and said, "It doesn't matter to us, dear, in what religion you raise this darling baby: Jewish or Christian! Just raise her so that she'll believe in God."

The extraordinary intelligence and humanity of Pista's mother, who only went to school for six short years and lived and died in a small Hungarian village she shared with just a few hundred people, taught me a true lesson of love and tolerance. Through her, I also learned to understand that Pista's world was not altered by his studies, by his new experiences, and by his new impressions; rather it remained his own. It remained the world he kept in his heart, one where he felt at home all his life.

11

The Railed Cot

The political tension created by Hungary's possible affiliation with the Soviet Union relaxed after a while. Stalin became more concerned with other issues; it seemed that the further enlargement of the Soviet Republic had lost its primacy for the moment. In fact, Hungary was not forced to join the Soviet Union: the massive population transfer that we feared never came to pass. Nonetheless, his aggression against the Jews and the oppression of the population intensified. Official antisemitism became widespread, and the regime became ever more aggressive.

On the other hand, my life with Pista continued to be miraculously beautiful: we were deeply in love with one another emotionally, spiritually, and physically. Intoxicated by each other's presence, we continued to live our daily lives as before: he went to classes at the university, worked at the observatory to earn some money, and prepared for his doctoral exams. I continued to take piano lessons from György Sebők, my teacher at the Béla Bartók Music School. Pressed by financial problems, we still lived happily at home with my parents in our beautiful apartment.

* * *

At the time we got married, I was still sleeping in my brother's former cot. He had graduated to a bed on his thirteenth birthday (two years before the German occupation of Hungary). Until then Iván had a white cot with rails, which he got at the age of three but which was long enough for a fifteen-year-old or even an older teenager. After he passed thirteen, however, I inherited his railed cot, and my parents bought him a new bed. Although the rails had not been taken off the cot, they didn't need to be pulled up either after I climbed into it every night; rather, they were left on the side of the cot. I slept in it for years to come. After the war, my parents had no money to buy a new bed for me, so even after our wedding, Pista and I continued to sleep in the same cot and, of course, in the same room where I had slept before my marriage. It took three years and my father's invention of a new medicine—for which he miraculously got a little bit of money—before my parents could afford to rebuild both my father's old bed and my mother's divan into one double bed so that now they had a new comfortable place to sleep and could afford to buy one larger bed for us as well. This was the time when we sold my railed cot. But we always remembered where we had slept for the first three years of our marriage. In fact, Pista often mentioned it even after we settled in America and could buy for ourselves as many beds as we wanted.

"Let's never forget where we came from: your railed cot."

12

Quiet Happiness

For the first year of our marriage we saw one another typically on Sundays, but sometimes Pista would come for the whole weekend, staying until Monday morning, when he would leave for the observatory again. Whether he came for a little while or stayed overnight, we always celebrated our happiness, feeling lucky that we met, fell in love, and were so happy! Pista would listen to me practicing the piano and eagerly looked forward to the chamber music nights that took place in our house almost every weekend. My father played in a string quartet whose members came to play every Saturday afternoon. Pista would listen to them with rapt attention. Instead of sitting in a chair, however, sometimes he would lie under the piano, writing mathematical formulae. I was constantly aware of his amazing ability of concentration when studying mathematics, his drawing of geometrical forms, his interesting way of making his thoughts visible, and his great delight in doing so. In addition, he had long discussions with my father about Hungarian history and the role the Russians played in Europe; these were discussions to which I listened closely. I admired the clarity of Pista's thinking, his penetrating intelligence, his humor, and his courageous understanding of the hopeless situation in which we found ourselves in Russian-occupied Hungary. Yet despite the cruel political world surrounding us, he did not give into despair; as a matter of fact he cherished life. We met with our friends, went to concerts and theatre performances, and told one another stories about everything that took place during the days we were not together.

I was delighted to see his pleasure in hearing my stories, telling him again and again that I had never met a person who took such interest and pleasure in another person's life and experience as he with mine. But he was so modest and so shy that when I talked about him and about his reactions to me, his response was puzzled:

"Why do you mention it? There is nothing special in what I just said!"

But there was! He relived all the events he heard from me as if he had personally experienced them, enjoying the good ones and becoming disturbed by the bad ones. Unfortunately, the latter almost always followed our discussions about the political pressure and the general despair which threatened our everyday life in Hungary. But the good stories made him happy: he would want to embrace the whole world.

13

Under Terror

At first Pista had a good time at the observatory; but after a while the stories he told me about his new workplace grew darker. Sure, there were good reasons for his having chosen to work there. People at the observatory did not feel the pressure of the Communist Party as directly as people in the departments of mathematics and physics at the university. There were reasons for this, too. By 1948 and 1949, in every possible respect the Hungarian Communist Party had started to rule the country with a brutality that is quite difficult to imagine today. Unlike reports on the skeletons and ashes discovered after the war in the German concentration camps and the mass graves at Babi Yar, there had been relatively little documentation in the Western press about the victims of Communist mass murders and Soviet occupation. But these were no secret to the population living under the Soviets. We heard, of course, about the many victims arrested and tortured in the country's prisons. And today we know that between 1948 and 1956 about 350,000 were involved in purges in Hungary, and another hundred thousand were forcefully "resettled" in the countryside. For most people living in this country, life turned into nightmare.

First of all there were the show trials. József Mindszenty, László Rajk, and a number of other leading political, cultural, or religious figures were accused of treason and of spying for the capitalists. These people were innocent, singled out because of their profession, background, or opinion, and they were tortured, sentenced to years of prison, or killed. Everyone lived in fear of the new terror. And then there was an enormous attack on the Jews—not only under Stalin's rule in the Soviet Union, where upon his order thousands were killed or deported to Siberia, but in the countries of the Soviet allies as well. For example, Dr. László Benedek, our neighbor in the apartment house on 10 Abonyi Street, who was the director of the Jewish Hospital in Budapest, was thrown into jail. He was not the only one: so were a number of Jewish doctors—following Stalin's order of arrests during and after the so-called "doctor trials" in the Soviet Union—and a number of Jewish politicians, many of them old communists and old social democrats were killed. In addition, people with no specific backgrounds—including several of our friends and acquaintances—were arrested and imprisoned, among them a friend of mine from school. She had been told by another sixteen-year-old on a streetcar that her class in school had to write an essay about Stalin. At this point the first girl mockingly imitated the "official voice" of radio announcers: "No! Not Stalin! Stalin Gen-er-al-is-si-mo!" At the next station she was arrested and taken to prison by the police, where they beat her up and kept her for several weeks.

But most arrests were made among the peasants, former military personnel, and members of the former higher middle and upper classes. Also, academics had been constantly checked and threatened in the early 1950s. Frightened of the danger and hoping to be left alone to do their own academic work, some joined the "commissars" who overran the universities, threatening others and demanding ever tighter obedience to the rulings of the Party. A few professors obliged because they hoped for a better life if they followed the Party's directions; others did so because they wanted more power. Yet others obeyed because they knew that under the circumstances resistance was not possible. This created a world in which those who joined the Party were running the universities as well, directing the participation of the individual departments. Many were willing to serve because they had directions from above and were afraid of rejecting the call. Others just wanted to be left alone and hoped for some freedom after satisfying the commands of the Party, believing that they would then be allowed to live as they wished, at least professionally. And, of course, there were some who wanted to become independent from those who ordered them around, thinking they would be able to achieve autonomy by obeying both the political and the bureaucratic order. Others cooperated because they were afraid of demotion if they did not do whatever was expected of them.

Enrolling in 1947 at the Eötvös Loránd University and majoring in mathematics and physics, Pista met a large number of world-famous mathematicians and enrolled in their classes: Lipót Fejér, Frigyes Riesz, Pál Turán, Alfréd Rényi, and others. Humble as he was, he told me that he was spellbound when he arrived; he could not believe that this was real, that these professors, these great, world-famous mathematicians were to be his teachers. He went to their classes, studied day and night, and it was not long before they became interested in him. Each wanted Pista to become an assistant in the institution he headed. First, however, he had to take certain exams before this was possible. He took them and passed each with distinction.

As time passed, however, the Communist pressure intensified in the country, becoming quite unbearable. It was perhaps no coincidence that the storm raged wildest in the countryside and at the universities.

While there were some professors who were not particularly involved or active in politics, many of their graduate students or assistants were forced to act in accordance with the directives of the Party. In fact it was the Party that organized the students in every department. Pista did not want to be organized by anybody, nor did he want to be politically active. He tried his best to disappear into the background not only because he wanted remove himself from the watching eyes of the Party but also because he wanted to be left alone to study mathematics. This was difficult, however. People had their eyes on him. It is true that his father was defined as a kulak and, therefore, as an "enemy of the people," who had to be sent to a prison for his "resistance" to turning over all of his produce to the state. Still, several politically minded people at the university looked upon Pista "with hope" as he came from a "peasant background" and they believed in the possibility of his "re-education," which could mean that after he "developed politically in the right direction" he could help them realize the ideal of a "newly born, socialist Hungary based on workers and peasants." He was told this several times by a number of Party members. But they failed to judge the situation correctly: Pista was never interested and would never be active in any realization of political ideas in Hungary or anywhere else. He wanted to be left in peace. There were only a few things he wanted to live for: mathematics, our marriage, and later our family.

By the time I got to know him, he could barely deal with the pressure. How could he continue his studies in mathematics as he would have liked to do? His other question was just as urgent: "Will I be able to stay in the field of mathematics if I work at the university?"—which was too public and too much under the eyes of the Party with its bureaucratic and politically active offices. Pista began to worry about his future.

One day he decided to talk to István Földes, associate professor in the department of astronomy. Pista knew and thought highly of him, partly because Földes was an intelligent and kind man and partly because Pista saw him as having tried to help people at the university who had been attacked for their bourgeois background. In addition, Pista had heard from several of his colleagues that Földes had saved a number of Jews in 1944 during the German occupation of Hungary.

They started to meet regularly. Going out one day for an espresso, Pista told Földes the problem he was facing: he wanted to study math but feared he would be unable to do this at the university, where Party members would try to involve him in politics. Also, he feared he would be constantly watched by them. What should he do? Apply for a research scholarship at the university? Would he remain free of the growing pressure of the Communist Party in either the mathematics or the physics department? Which of these two would be better? Are institutions outside that particular campus as closely watched and checked or as vulnerable? Should he try the observatory? If he went into astronomy, would he still have to work on the university campus? Wouldn't the observatory be the simplest goal for him?

Földes agreed. "That's a good way to look at things," the older Pista told the younger one, who later told me about this discussion that took place a few months before I got to know him. "Those people on the mountain" (Földes meant the astronomers, since the observatory was placed on one of the high hills surrounding Budapest) "aren't crazy *Communist* maniacs; you'll be able to spend your time in a more quiet, almost apolitical milieu. It's what I would do in your place."

What this meant was that if Pista went into the field of astronomy, he could work at the Institute of Astronomy, located far away from the university on the top of Buda's highest hill, Szabadság-hegy ("Mountain of Freedom," as the new system had renamed it). This was an observatory led by the well-known astronomer László Detre and joined by several research scholars, including a number of graduate students and a few mechanical workers who kept the equipment running. These scholars seemed to live the life Pista was looking for, free from the pressures of everyday politics and doing whatever they wanted professionally. Indeed "the people on the mountain" appeared to be free from the restrictions imposed upon the personnel at the university: neither the director nor the observatory's other researchers were members of the Communist Party—except one, who was completely harmless. The name of this young man was Tibor Herczeg. He had also been a student at Eötvös College and the university. Perhaps at first, when the "new religion" started to overtake Hungary's intellectual circles, he had been a believer in communism, but by the early 1950s Tibor had turned away from politics, becoming ever more aware of the misdeeds of the Party and using his membership mainly to help others.

Yet even before he fully recognized the destruction the Communist Party unleashed on the country, Tibor would never have harmed anyone, especially a colleague. In fact, to the great amusement of his friends, even during the worst Stalinist terror, Tibor worried about the future consequences of his own Party membership.

"What will happen to me if the world changes and the Russians disappear? Would I be persecuted for having been a member of the Party?" He kept on asking his non-Communist colleagues these questions—outrageously absurd though! They were in Hungary in the early 1950s, at the zenith of the Party's power and Russia's influence in Hungary. There was no sign whatsoever pointing to any possible political change.

Otherwise there were no communist scholars or workers at the observatory. Hence while political tensions created a disturbing way of life in the Russian-occupied part of the world and, of course, at virtually every Hungarian scientific institution, they were practically nonexistent in the Budapest Observatory.

More than that, this was a place where no one had to fear pressure from the regime. No one. It was obvious that if Pista could go there, he would be left in peace. He could do whatever he wanted to do. Nobody would go after him. First of all, in contrast to the university, in the observatory there was no dangerous Party secretary who would check up on people. Second, there was no push in this institution to force its members to go to Party meetings; they were not expected to receive ever changing ideological instructions, observe other people, or write reports denouncing one another.

When the observatory on the mountain offered Pista a fellowship, he was very happy. Of course, he knew that deciding to go there, he would need to find a dissertation topic in astronomy rather than in mathematics. Although it was mathematics rather than astronomy he wanted to study, he thought that for the time being it would be possible for him to write a dissertation in astronomy and return to mathematics after he had a secure job somewhere else and could do whatever he liked. He did not yet know that this was more of a dream than a real plan, nor did he realize the negative side of involving himself in vast areas of work about which he was not passionate. Unfortunately, ignorant as I was in this area, I also played a role in his decision. I wanted him to be left alone and to live without outside disturbances. Földes and others convinced me that working at the observatory would assure him of this. It was a way of life I thought that Pista needed more than anyone. I encouraged him to accept it.

It was a mistake, however. We were both inexperienced and naïve. Pista had no immediate idea what his decision would mean—and neither did I. Nor did he know for sure what else to do. He did not ask himself what he was most passionate about. He only considered what appeared to be "reasonable" and "practical" to him: the prospect of being left alone. But his desire to study mathematics was stronger and more intense than the practical solution he thought would resolve his problem. He was thus not happy with the work he volunteered to undertake, and for as long as he worked in astronomy he never stopped longing to go back to mathematics.

There was another problem confronting him on the mountain. It was certainly less intense than his professional concerns, yet it never ceased to disturb and even annoy him as long as he worked there—from 1951 to the end of November 1956.

On the one hand he was on very good terms with his colleagues, including the director László Detre, who thought highly of him. There was also Detre's wife and co-worker Júlia Balázs, and another very intelligent young man, Imre Izsák, a classmate of Pista's at the university as well as a colleague of his at Eötvös College. In addition, there was the aforementioned Tibor Herczeg, another young astronomer and the Party secretary at Budapest Observatory. There were three other scholars too, but they were reserved and held back from the rest for some reason. Pista did not have much direct contact with them. With Detre, Balázs, Herczeg, and Izsák, however, he had a close relationship. The five of them spent many hours discussing scholarly topics as well as politics, especially Soviet rule over Hungary, the country's tragic participation in World War II, and its fall into the hands of Communist Russia. These kinds of discussions were ongoing at that time in Hungary, with virtually everybody aware of the new and catastrophically brutal political dictatorship. People often became intensely involved with one another after such discussions about the system under which all Hungarians had to live. They formed part of the observatory's coffee breaks, lunch breaks, and other social occasions; colleagues were constantly chatting, arguing, and sometimes even agreeing with one another.

At first Pista enjoyed these discussions: at last he could speak freely, say what he thought, and did not have to fear the consequences of taking a stance against the system. This gave him a sense of freedom he had not had in his last two years at Eötvös College or at the university. As a matter of fact, students had been under increasing pressure at these institutions: they had to take compulsory Marxism-Leninism classes, learn Russian (no matter how many other languages they already spoke), and clap when they were told to clap. They had to be constantly on guard as to what they said or what other students said in front of them because denouncements were rampant on campus. In addition, it was hard to get away from the Party line. One could not read, listen to the radio, or look at a newspaper without being confronted by the demands and threats of the Party or "the news," which was defined as the only true news. Everything else, especially criticism of the system, was declared to be "coming from the enemy."

Initially the discussions in the observatory relieved Pista's tension and anxiety, living as we all did under continual pressure. But after a while he began to grow concerned. The discussions on the mountain revolved not only around the oppressive system of communism in Hungary but also around the "damage the Jews had caused the country." Obviously, like most people, Pista's colleagues were outraged by the brutality and violence of the Communist system, but as true antisemites (except Tibor Herczeg, who hated antisemitism) they understood the Communist doctrine and the Communist practice just as the Nazis had promulgated for years—as a violation of the country's population by a "Jewish conspiracy." In fact, blaming the Jews for Russian communism as well as for "world communism" and the development of Hungarian socialism and socialist ideas, these astronomers defined the Jews within the framework of the Nazi concepts: as the creators of evil in the world. In fact, like many adherents of the antisemitic Right, they saw the rise of socialism and communism as the result of ideas inherent in Jewish thinking and, most importantly, inherent in the Jewish desire to rule the world. Hence they saw political events and developments in terms of "the Jewish laws," referring to the relatively large Jewish participation in the development of Marxist theory and the buildup of the new Hungarian takeover of power by the Party. These discussions were deeply antisemitic, blaming the Jews for both the Soviet and the Hungarian Communist terror, painting them as responsible for the mass murders taking place in Soviet-occupied Eastern and Central Europe and elsewhere.

It is true that in 1919 half of the so-called Communist commissars who created the Communist dictatorship in Hungary under the direction of Béla Kun were of Jewish origin. But they were, of course, not Jewish. Unless we think of the world in racial terms, we have no basis to define them as Jews. First of all they denied and refused any relationship to the Jews. Declaring themselves socialists or communists rather than Jewish, they had nothing to do with the Jewish religious tradition, Jewish ideas, or Jewish philosophical thought. Nor had they identified themselves as culturally Jewish. Hence unless we believe in racial theories and in what the Nazis called "the voice of the blood," these people were not Jewish. There can be no doubt that by the middle of the nineteenth and the beginning of the twentieth century in some countries, especially in Russia's Pale of Settlement, where five million Jews lived—most of them in utter poverty—some saw the possibility of creating a new world in which equality rather than class systems and religious prejudice would prevail. Pariahs themselves for centuries, having lived under the constant threat of pogroms and discrimination, a number of people born into Jewish families but separating themselves from their ancestors and turning their backs on their tradition identified with the rest of the population and started to believe that they could improve the world by spreading socialism. This movement grew in both numbers and force by the end of World War I. In 1919 after the fall of the Communist government in Hungary, several people born as Hungarian Jews fled to the Soviet Union. If they survived Stalin's purges during the 1930s, they returned to Hungary after 1945 and became participants and activists in the political process the Communist Party created in the country. But the idea that Jews were guilty of the creation of communism in the world was as absurd as earlier accusations of the Nazis describing the "Jewish enemy," an accusation which has poisoned the relationship between Jews and Christians for two millennia.

Since the crimes of the Communist government during 1919 were not easily forgotten by the population of Hungary, they often appeared in everyday discussion among people talking about the recent rules, comparing them to those of the past. Such discussions took place daily in the observatory. At first this was not a problem. Living under the pressure of the Stalinist terror, people were relieved finally to have found a place where they could speak openly to one another. In fact, Pista had been happy to talk freely. But after a while he felt increasingly alienated by listening to

Figure 6. Pista and I in Germany (probably 1958).

what he described as "those terrible antisemitic discussions on the mountain."

Could Pista have stood up during these discussions and left the room? Of course. But he would have had to face the reactions to such a stance—a hostile environment in which it would have been very hard to live and work. Also, at this point, it would have been very difficult to sever the relationship he had built with his colleagues. Having chosen astronomy as his major, he no longer had a place to return to. In other words, he did not have a choice. The semester had started. He had to prepare for his exams and begin writing his dissertation.

As he told me very sadly, "My only hope is that despite everything, we'll survive!"

But he was quite unhappy in this milieu, and it did not help him to know that he had no choice. While the university was too big, too powerful, and too much under the influence of the Communist Party, the observatory was too small, too aggressive, and too antisemitic for him to accept it as a tolerable environment. The situation started to become burdensome for both of us. And there was no hope for change. After a while, however, as always when difficulties arose, Pista learned to live with the thought that having made a choice, good or bad, he must continue to accept it—at least for the moment.

Although, as he told me, he was often quite disturbed during the day, when he came home he could forget what had happened in the office and enjoy our life.

14

Living for the Moment

At home everything seemed as beautiful as it could be. We loved one another ever more. Our three-and-a-half-room apartment on Otto Hermann Street, where my parents lived with Erzsi, Iván, and later his wife Mari, in addition to Pista and me, did not seem crowded or uncomfortable. The villa had four apartments. All of them opened to a garden sprinkled with flowerbeds and rosebushes, facing the high hills where the observatory was located. The truth is that we were grateful to live in such a wonderful place. In fact, Pista was always grateful: grateful for our home and our life in Hungary, grateful later to leave for Germany, grateful to come to America, grateful to be able to work in the fields of theoretical physics, grateful for our children, grateful for our jobs. He was a humble, happy man who never forgot where he came from and how good our life turned out to be. And while at that time he recognized the fragility of our existence in Hungary, he was also aware of our happiness and hoped for a time that we could live in a place where we would be free.

* * *

Even during the early fifties, amidst misery and constant financial stress, we were aware of and enjoyed our good fortune, loving one another as deeply as we did and living in such a beautiful place. In this way a great need of mine was satisfied, which stemmed perhaps from my experience in Budapest during the siege and after the war when we continued to live in a city which was demolished by the Allies. At that time the mere need for living space was an enormously pressing problem in Budapest, and most people's hope of being able to resolve this problem seemed completely futile. Between November 1944 and February 1945 most of the city's streets and most of its houses had been destroyed by the Allies' twenty-four hour bombardment, in addition to the Soviets' heavy artillery and perpetual mortar fire, devastating Budapest for four long months. In fact, according to historians Budapest had been one of the ten most bombed cities of World War II. Its rebuilding came very slowly, taking decades—mostly because there were no funds or means to rebuild. As a result, Hungary's capitol could not hide its terrible wounds of destruction and was forced for many decades to house hundreds of thousands of people, who had to live two or three families to an apartment of two or three rooms, often with only one toilet, no heating, no kitchen, and sometimes no bathroom.

Our family was lucky. Our first apartment house on Abonyi Street, where we moved in 1941, was not bombed during the Siege of Budapest—unlike most buildings in the city. Erzsi had moved in during the last months of the siege. What she achieved by simply being there was that our furniture had neither been stolen nor burned in the neighbors' stove. The lack of coal during the cold winter of 1944 moved many people to burn the furniture of Jews who had had to leave their apartments.

We moved back to this apartment after the war. Of course, all its windows were broken from the four month siege, and even after we had replaced them, ruins, dust, and dirt created by the bombing nearby covered everything. It was not the same place we had lived in before the war. Yet our general poverty did not allow us to fix the damage. But then, we were lucky again. In 1949 the Hungarian Ministry of Interior Affairs decided to expropriate the house on Abonyi Street where we had lived for eight years and declared itself willing to pay for the move of all the tenants. In other words, everybody who resided in this house had to move out within a week and find a new apartment, leaving behind this "old" one, which had been set aside for several members of the new Hungarian government. While this was a terrible hassle, by mere chance my mother found another beautiful place in Buda. With our thousands of books, my six-foot Steinway piano, and the library furniture created years before by the famous designer Sándor Kolozsvári, we moved into the new apartment: it was on Otto Hermann Street, one of four other apartments in a house on Buda's "Rosehill," opposite the "Mountain of Freedom" where István's observatory was located. We were living in this apartment when we married in 1950, and it was in this apartment that we stayed while we lived in Hungary. As time passed, however, despite our great personal happiness, we agonized about the future. In fact, at times I was driven by confusion and fear.

What will happen to us? How will I become a great pianist if I won't be accepted again at the Music Academy? Am I good enough? Why would they accept me now? When will Pista finish his dissertation in astronomy, and how will he become a mathematician again? As a matter of fact, will he ever be able to return to mathematics? Isn't he losing time doing something he doesn't really want to do? Where will he get a job? Will my father and mother be always as desperate as they are now, never forgetting about what we have gone through during the Holocaust? Will they never forget about the loss of their brothers and sisters? For the moment we can live with my parents, but can we always? And how can they overcome the financial loss we suffered during the German occupation? And now, during the time of the Communist era? Will we always be hungry? Lacking nice clothing? Will we never be able to look forward to a good future?

I was gasping for an answer to these questions—at times thinking that even to frame them made no sense whatsoever. Listening to people more experienced than I was, I understood that the Russians would never go away, and our life would always remain the same. Whenever I thought about this, I would become truly desperate.

First of all, I was often very hungry; after 1949 we never had enough to eat. When I thought of the food I loved and which we simply could not buy, I had to face the fact that we did not have—and perhaps never would have—enough money to buy it. In desperation I would go to the kitchen in search

Figure 7. A small part of our library in Budapest.

Figure 8. My Steinway.

of food, and if I found some beans or potatoes I would eat and become less desperate, trying not to think about chocolate cake because if I did, I would cry. Sometimes I would go and look in shop windows filled with food and imagine that I was eating. It helped a bit.

And sometimes, I just went to look at the same silver purse, black blouse, or purple dress that were in the shop windows for weeks (often for months). For I was not only hungry for food; I had no nice clothes to wear for many years after the end of the war. And when I thought about clothes or food, I feared I would never have either again.

Also, by the end of the 1940s, our apartment on Abonyi Street had begun to lose its former glamour. If something like the water heater in the bathroom stopped working, we could not have it fixed; we had no money. That meant we could not take a bath. We would wash ourselves in the kitchen in a washbowl. And we could not heat all the rooms in the apartment, just two of them. In 1953 Pista decided to learn Russian in order to translate books on astronomy into Hungarian. With translation he could make some money, but it slowed down the progress of his dissertation. As a matter of fact, our life in Hungary in the early fifties was almost as miserable as it had been during the Siege of Budapest. Of course, no bombs were falling, and we were not being persecuted, especially if I kept my mouth shut, but still the past seemed to be repeating itself. Or had it never gone away at all?

As soon as I tried to formulate these thoughts, I saw everything falling apart. It was the same image I had seen during the Holocaust. Not only did we live in poverty, but whenever my father was late for supper I would be afraid that he had been arrested, put into jail, and I would not see him again. My memories of the Holocaust returned and started to seem real. Pista's strong presence helped me a great deal, but if for some reason he was not home, or if I could not get hold of him at his office, I would imagine that he, too, had been arrested, tortured, and murdered.

Pista, on the other hand, was despite of everything always well-balanced and happy.

"We have one another," he would tell me again and again, "and we always will."

But this did not assuage my fears and nightmares. I constantly felt threatened. To me, life was hard for us again, and no betterment was in sight. At this point, I attempted to forget about the future: I simply decided to halt the passage of time.

15

Playmates

A few weeks after I met Pista, I introduced him to the group of my friends and playmates, my "Winnie the Pooh Partners" we all read the story of *Winnie the Pooh* as teenagers or young adults and it made a deep impression on each of us. My friends Julika, Éva, Katalin, Maca, and Ottó were later joined by Vica and her husband, the well-known pianist György Sebők, my teacher and friend.

I had met Julika Kerpel first. One day her mother visited my father, whom she knew from "better times," hoping to find a job with his help. Ever since 1948, when the state "nationalized" their pharmacy (known in Budapest as "the Kerpel Pharmacy"), she had worked in a factory. This was the year when all pharmacies and businesses were nationalized in Hungary, and since she did not have a profession and her husband had been killed in the Holocaust, the Kerpels became destitute. Although my father could not get her a job, during her visit with him she met and invited me to their home to meet her daughter, Julika.

Originally Julika Kerpel was interested in psychology, but being the daughter of the owner of one of Budapest's largest and most famous pharmacies, she had not been accepted as a student in the psychology department at the university. The Party gave preference to the applications of young men and women from working-class families rather than those whom it classified as children of a capitalist background. Giving up the idea of psychology as her major, she enrolled in the children's therapy education department, where she had been accepted together with some other first-year students who had also been refused by the Communist overseers of the psychology department. Julika did not mind the change. In fact, fearing the uncertainty of university life, she and most of her classmates were satisfied with the school in which they would continue their studies. Also, some renowned psychologists teaching in this department made the change of schools not only acceptable but highly positive. Later in life, when she finally left Hungary, she enrolled in medical school in London and became a psychiatrist in Switzerland.

Julika and I were truly close friends. Our relationship was similar to those I had had with my playmates in the ghetto house where I'd lived during the German occupation, playing fantasy games day and night. At first I thought that this had happened to me alone and to the particular group of children living in our ghetto house. But as I found out much later, there were many similar children's groups all over the city who had done the same. In fact, as I was told later while talking with friends about these groups, it was as if a "playing bee" had stung the children of the ghetto houses during the summer and fall of 1944 and during the Siege of Budapest. The anti-Jewish, war-ridden, life-threatening city became one large playground for children, many of whom were playing fantasy games. And their desire to continue with these games did not fade when the war ended. It stayed with most of them for as long as they lived in Hungary. After leaving the country, however, most of us realized that we had to change, since these kinds of games for young adults were quite unknown in other parts of the world. As a result, with time and travel, the urge to play fantasy games faded away in each of us. But in Budapest we played these charades with one another—giving in to an urge that probably grew out of our need to create

Figure 9. Pista and a group of astronomers in the Soviet Union (1953).

a world for ourselves where we could flee from the danger threatening our physical existence at every moment.

I met Julika in 1952 and we parted in 1956, eventually fleeing from Hungary in different directions. But during our time in Budapest we played endlessly. There was always at least one person acting out roles while the other person or the rest of the group had to figure out which play, novel, or poem these roles came from. Sometimes we invented plays that gave a different ending to *Romeo and Juliet* or *King Lear* or *Othello* or *Faust*; other times we acted as characters we invented or as characters from "real life": we were true lovers, betrayed husbands, insulted wives, angry children, disappointed citizens, Germans, Russians, great painters, musicians, pianists, or conductors. Often we recited poems to one another and accompanied them with music while some of us tried to identify who wrote or composed a particular piece. Also we drew caricatures, attempting to identify artists, politicians, poets; or we recited texts out of plays, trying to figure out the authors. Meeting new friends always meant that we had new people to play with, helping our attempts at fleeing the present.

Julika had curly brown hair and beautiful large eyes, and she specialized in the role of the deceived bride. Her life was far from easy, however. Having lost her father in the Holocaust, she often talked about him and was wracked by terrible pain and sadness. But she also had tremendous strength and an intense desire to overcome the wound her father's murder had opened, trying to surmount the horrors that marked her difficult life and that of her mother. Julika wanted to live freely, to learn, and to experience the world at its fullest and happiest while being constantly aware of the tragedy that had befallen them. She wanted to fall in love, to marry, to forget her burden, and to live a normal life. Hoping to find her heart's desire, she often fell in love with men with some deeply poetic inclinations who were tall, thin, blue-eyed, and blond . She read lyrics in several languages and the novels and other writings of the great writers in addition to studying day and night for her classes. Transfixed by the depth and power of literature, art, psychology, and our games, she became one of the closest friends of my life.

My other best friend was Éva, the daughter of one of Hungary's greatest musicologists, Bence Szabolcsi, who came from a well-known Jewish literary family. As a Jew, Szabolcsi was silenced for twenty-five years in Hungary—first during the Horthy era (1919–44) and then, like every other Hungarian Jew, he was persecuted during the German occupation. But even before, during the Horthy era of active antisemitism and anti-Jewish laws, Jews could neither be public servants nor could they hold a job with the state. Szabolcsi earned a living by writing about music in Jewish newspapers and books during the 1920s and 1930s. He became professor of musicology at the Franz Liszt Music Academy after the war in 1945. During the German occupation, however, he was not only jobless, but like every Jew at the time he faced constant danger for his life. Hiding during the Holocaust in Budapest, Szabolcsi, his wife Klári, and his daughter Éva managed to stay alive, as did half of the two hundred thousand Jews of Budapest. But his thirteen-year-old son Gábor did not. Catching a streetcar in May 1944 (an action which was forbidden for Jews except during the day between 10:00 A.M. and 12:00 P.M.—the only time they were allowed to buy food and appear in the streets), Gábor left the ghetto house at precisely at 10:00 A.M., the hour he was allowed to do so. He decided to go to Buda, to their tiny lot where some fruit trees grew. This was the place he always visited in the spring to pick a few cherries from their cherry tree and take them home. But this time he was caught in the streetcar by two Hungarian gendarmes. Like every Jew had to wear in public, he was wearing a canary-yellow star on the left-hand side of his coat, as ordered by the new Hungarian law. That he was in a streetcar at a time when he was allowed to be there did not keep the gendarmes from acting brutally: they picked him up and took him to the concentration camp in Kistarcsa. From there the young boy was deported to Auschwitz a few weeks later, and after a short while he was killed in the camp.

Éva wanted to become a theater director, but she spent only one year in the College of Dramatic Art in Budapest. After her second semester she was advised not to continue in this field. In fact only a handful of students were allowed to do so. These decisions were completely arbitrary, however, made on the basis of political guidelines rather than talent and interest in the field. Desperate and disappointed, Éva enrolled in Italian studies at the university, translating over the years a number of plays and beautiful Italian poems into Hungarian.

Éva was always the most marvelous character in the games in which the three of us played the main roles. In addition, she was a warm, loving soul and the most loyal friend I have ever known. Her golden hair cascaded onto her shoulders and her sky-blue eyes lit up her thin, beautifully expressive, intelligent face. I have never known anyone who played fantasy games with such dedication and who took friendship so seriously and treated it with such a devotion as she did. After we left Hungary we met several times in the late 1960s and early 1970s, including once in Rome and once in Venice, the two Italian cities that played a major part in our games in Budapest, the two cities where all of us longed to go and live one day. Éva fell in love with a famous Italian conductor. She died in the 1980s of heart failure.

Katalin was significantly older than we were. In her late thirties during our friendship in the early 1950s, she had blue eyes; brown hair; and a beautifully-drawn, noble face. She had to support, however, her fourteen-year-old daughter Bori. Katalin hoped to earn a diploma from the Béla Bartók School of Music in order to teach piano and voice in school. But one day she lost her scholarship and was left alone with Bori without a penny in the world. Secretly, all of her friends put together our pocket money—and the money we earned doing this and that—and for the next fifteen months we supported the two girls until Katalin received her diploma, found a job, and started teaching.

Another member of the group was Maca, a pianist like me, also a student of Sebők. Hoping to be accepted at the music academy, she practiced day and night and played beautifully. Tall and thin with dark, passionate eyes and an exquisitely shaped face, Maca was not only spectacularly beautiful but also an extraordinarily intelligent and warm-hearted human being. Yet she had a very hard fate and suffered tremendously. Her father had been killed in the winter of 1944 to1945, at the time of the Siege of Budapest. During the heavy bombardment of the city the walls of their house collapsed and fell on him. At this point, she was twelve years old. Shortly after his death, Maca was raped by three Russian soldiers. She and her mother worked, but they didn't always succeed in bringing the money together they needed for the month. Maca tried to practice eight to ten hours a day, though, for her entrance concert to the music academy. Finally, she was accepted. But after receiving her diploma, she did not become a concert pianist. There was no room for most gifted people in that stiflingly unjust, cruel political system of Hungary during the 1950s and 1960s, just for a few lucky ones; rather, she taught music in a music school for very little money and continued to live a hard and difficult life. She died of lung cancer in 1988 at the age of fifty-six.

Another member of our group was Otto Till, a tall, blond, lanky violinist and conductor who had joined the military in order to earn his living during these hard times. He was for a while the crown prince of Julika's colorful imagination and the object of her love. But this affair was more an imaginary than a real relationship. Otto was a religious Catholic, and he was interested in things other than love. He had constant pangs of conscience about playing the role of the Communist soldier in the Hungarian army rather than showing his contempt for—and his fear of—the system in which we lived. Wracked by these conflicts, he was not interested in affairs of the heart, at least for the moment. Strangely enough, however, he played along with us when it came to our games, happily identifying himself with Winnie the Pooh or the Little Prince, or he would take on the role of Raskolnyikov, the hero of Dostoevsky's *Crime and Punishment*, or King László V in the Arany poem.

A few years later, our group was joined by György and Vica Sebők. She was a funny, sweet, intelligent, lovely woman with brown hair and beautiful brown eyes, and he an extremely intelligent man and famous pianist in Budapest, who moved to the United States in the late 1950s and became a professor of piano at Indiana University. He concertized as a soloist and became the pianist partner of the famous cellist János Starker, also of Hungarian heritage. Both Vica and Gyuri participated in our games, playing along as well as inventing new ones. They became very close to all of us, ready to play an important role in our "children's group." With them we also acted in short theater plays as well as new performance pieces we wrote ourselves.

Naturally, Pista, too, was a member of this group, just as if he had grown up among us, listening to our chamber music concerts, while lying on the floor under the piano and doing mathematics. Whenever he took a break, he played fantasy and theater games with us, always coming up with new ideas. At our last performance, on Vica's birthday sometime in 1956, I remember, he played a court astronomer, dressed in a silver gown and a red hat. He also told stories about the stars and the universe, acting out trips to the planets and to the Moon way before the first men appeared there. We pretended to go along and sang him songs during these trips. But other times he just sat amidst us surrounded by papers and books, writing and listening to our games yet also staring at the walls and drawing mathematical formulae.

16

Dangerous Winds

Time passed rapidly. As political life deteriorated in Hungary and with it our sense of a future, we still were happy about being able to play, planning our weekly games, and avoiding the lives of "adults." Also, seeing what was happening in the larger world, we were happy to be left alone, avoiding punishment for who we were and what we thought. But we did not live in the real world. We knew that our fantasy games did not have a future. Most of the time we tried very hard not to think about what would happen to us when we had to "grow up."

Indeed we had to look at the world and ourselves when we could no longer be together. I, for example, started to give up all hope of ever being accepted at the Academy of Music. My father was the former owner of a pharmacy and a serum laboratory. That I would not get in was almost a certainty. I knew that the Party secretary of the Béla Bartók School of Music thought that I was "unreliable," using this word that the Party used to describe "the enemies of the people." So what would I do when I grew up? By that time I was over twenty. And what would happen to Pista? And his interest in mathematics?

* * *

As I have mentioned, in the early 1950s only my father was earning money in our family. Iván did not need to be supported any longer; he was on call at least twice a week, which made him self-sufficient. Pista had some income from the observatory as a PhD candidate. I, on the other hand, earned almost nothing. No doubt it was time to think about what would happen in the future. But the problem was that I could not think ahead because I felt that there were no possibilities for me to play piano and also earn money, thereby, improving our lives. I had not learned or studied anything except the piano. Of course, I could have taught more students. But had I done so, I feared, it would mean shortening my own practice hours significantly. The conflict was painful: how could I become a professional pianist yet practice less than I had been when this was all I wanted to accomplish in the world? And what about Pista? His working outside of mathematics would have meant giving up what he wanted to do more than anything. Discussion piled upon discussion; finally he decided to learn Russian. Although he already spoke German and Italian and wanted to do nothing more than study mathematics, he decided to translate some Russian texts on mathematics or astronomy into Hungarian because the Hungarian presses paid more for these translations than he could have earned as a graduate student. And since neither of us saw any possibility of my doing something else, except getting more piano students, he felt he was the one who had to pick up the pieces and learn Russian. Taking it with good humor and strength, within a few months he had learned several thousand of Russian words and begun the translation of an astronomy book originally published in Russian.

* * *

Then suddenly, disquieting news swept through the city. It happened during the months of June and July 1951 that a large number of families living in Budapest received letters from the Ministry of Interior Affairs individually assigning them to new living quarters in the houses of families who lived in distant villages. In fact, without being given any reason, these families were told that within twenty-four hours, they must leave their apartments in Budapest and register at a certain police station. From there, they were to be transported within forty-eight hours on trucks or by train to the towns assigned to them, where the police had secured places for them to live, one room per family. They would have to report weekly at the police station in the town they had been assigned to move to, where they would have to settle. At this point, they were allowed to go home to pack their suitcases, but they had also been warned to sign in within a day or two at the police station to which they were assigned.

People who received this letter, many of them former army officers and government employees, intellectuals, and aristocrats, had to appear with their families within twenty-four hours at a police station in Budapest, their money and jewelry left in the hands of their apartments' caretakers. The government didn't give any reason nor any excuse for this action. But it was obvious that besides planning to "punish the rich," this decision of the rulers was influenced by the enormous need for apartments in Budapest. A large number of houses had been bombed during the siege of the city, and the state had no money to build new ones or rebuild the old ones. Facing up to this dilemma, the leadership had found a "solution": to force people out of their homes and move in the regime's supporters. While tens of thousands of people were forced to move to the countryside, the "chosen ones" moved into "their" new apartments and lived there "happily ever after." And like the Jews who were driven out of their apartments in 1944, the displaced residents were never able to retrieve them. In fact the new victims of the 1950s were driven in trucks or taken by trains to the houses of the so-called kulaks, "rich peasants" who lived in faraway villages. What the deportees would live on without their monthly salaries, and what they would even be capable of doing under such circumstances, was not discussed. Tens of thousands had their apartments given to those whom the Party wished to reward for their "good work," while those who were deported were given the "right" to live in a house in the countryside in which a single room had been set aside for them, described as "the place of the newly arriving family." Of course, these people were removed not only from their apartments and taken to a foreign place but were also separated from their jobs, their incomes, and their own lives.

What was the real reason for this operation? In part the leadership wanted to provide apartments for members of the Party—especially those who were defined as reliable—living spaces that almost nobody could afford as they were scarce and cost a fortune even during the decades after the war. It also wanted to punish and finally get rid of all of those who had been successful during the previous regime, defining them as "enemies of the people."

I feared the worst because from 1945 to 1948, my father had owned both his pharmacy and serum lab. Every night I would shake with fear in Pista's arms. In fact he never fell asleep without reassuring me that whatever happened, the two of us would never be separated, nor would we be separated from my parents. He knew that from the time of the Holocaust my greatest dread was that we could be separated. All my life afraid of losing my father and our home, I was terrified of the future. Of course, I could not help but draw parallels between our lives during the German occupation and the life we were living at this point in Budapest. But Pista had significant power to calm me down. He repeated again and again that despite everything, as long as the authorities did not threaten us personally, as long as they did not single out our parents, we should concentrate on our work and enjoy our life and happiness. Was he that strong? Or was I so much afraid because I had lived through what the Germans had done, and I saw the similarities between the two regimes? I will never know, but he kept on repeating that as long as they did not separate us, our heaven would remain untouched. And he was right; despite everything, it remained untouched.

17

Deportations

Then one day at seven in the evening, I received a call from my friend Vera Madarász. She was crying bitterly, calling me from a public phone to tell me that her mother and stepfather were going to be deported the next morning from Budapest. She said she could not keep our appointment for that night because she had to help them move. I wanted to go to her and show her that she was not alone. I decided to help her move the furniture and books from her parents' apartment to hers. But when I told this to my father, he would not let me go. I was not allowed to risk my life for anybody in the world. As he said, "The police might come to pick up not only those chosen to be moved tomorrow but also Vera and you and anyone they might find there, and who knows what the future of such people would be?" I was afraid to call Pista: he was on the mountain and this was not a topic to be discussed on the phone, as the calls of ordinary citizens in Hungary were being tapped at this time. In addition, I feared that he, too, would tell me not to leave the house when I wanted to do so.

I waited for my parents to go to bed. When they fell asleep I left the house, taking a streetcar to Vera's; her parents lived close by. I was almost there—I even had a view of the house when I noticed someone coming through the entrance carrying a chair: it was Pista. I ran to him.

"What are you doing here?" I asked, beside myself, as if in a dream.

He answered as always, in a simple but very concrete way, "I heard from Imre" (a mutual friend) "about the impending deportation of Vera's parents, and I thought I would come and help."

God in heaven! He was my hero! He was my husband, my beloved, my companion! The fulfillment of my dreams! He would always help people when they were being persecuted; he would always help if the Germans came for us, just as he was helping now when the Communist government was threatening our friends! He would always help those who needed him! Since childhood this had been the criterion for me of a true friend, of a true human being! He came to help at a time of danger because his help was needed and because he did not want our dear friends to feel abandoned. As he told me later, he did not call me because he did not want to endanger me: he tried to help on his own.

After embracing in the street, we carried furniture, dishes, towels, and bedding back and forth all night—holding hands, kissing, and hugging one another again and again. Then we went home. We heard the next morning from Vera that after her parents walked to the police station, they were arrested and deported. Living for four years under miserable circumstances in one room of a farmer's tiny little house, they were finally allowed to return to Budapest. Of course, at this point, their apartment had been taken away from them, their pension had been erased (they were in their late sixties–early seventies) and they had no chance of getting a job. Stripped of their past and future alike, they died soon after their return.

18

A Decision

A couple of years passed. Pista was near to finishing his dissertation, and I was taking my final exams at the Béla Bartók School of Music. Of course, before my concert exam I had to pass my finals in other fields as well. Sitting on the floor with Maca for the fifth day, in the summer of 1955, we tried to learn 350 new folk songs, as we were expected to know all of them at our folk music exam. Folk music and folk songs were taken very seriously in Hungary at the time because the leadership wished to emphasize the importance of the "folk" in the Hungarian "People's Democracy." More important, however, Zoltán Kodály, the greatest living composer in Hungary, well-known all over the world, was convinced of the national, pedagogical, musical, and ethical importance of Hungarian folk music for the intellectual and emotional development of the country's youth. And although Kodály was not the Communist government's favorite ideological adherent—in fact he was a known opponent of the system—they let him do whatever he wanted in the realm of music. Kodály's major concern was to teach children the ancient Hungarian folk songs, compositions that completely differed from the nineteenth- and twentieth-century popular approaches of Western musical culture, which he wanted to eradicate from the country's musical consciousness. The Communist leadership liked this approach: Kodály was allowed to influence and decide on the courses music students had to take in Hungary. And despite the conflicts Kodály had with the Communist leadership, his program was respected and carried out by the music teachers in the country's schools as well as in its music academies. Thus students had to learn hundreds of folk songs every semester in the Hungarian music schools.

Sitting on the floor with Maca learning, repeating, and practicing one folk song after the other, most of which we did not know, I was driven crazy by my desire to practice the piano rather than prepare for this exam. Of course, every school of learning in every country of the world offers subjects that are not necessarily intertwined with subjects students want to study. I knew that. But this was worse than the usual problem. There was no argument, no dispute, no question of replacement regarding the issue: to pass this class, there were 350 folk songs to be studied for each semester, and there was no substitute class to be taken. Nor could the exam be postponed, nor the number of folk songs lowered. Period.

Hence, I sat with Maca on the floor, learning folk songs. My insides were raging: I wanted to practice Bach's *Chromatic Fantasy and Fugue*. It was resounding in my head, in my heart, in my fingers, and I wanted to play it splendidly: I needed to practice! The pressure was almost unbearable. Suddenly the bell rang. I got up and opened the door. It was the mailman. There in the mail was a letter from my good friend Éva Wimmer, who had fled with her mother from Hungary to Switzerland in 1947. I did not open it immediately but just looked at the envelope and held it in my hand.

I sat down and as if seeing a vision, I said, "Do you know, Maca, there are countries in the world where they never wore the yellow star? Countries where one's relatives weren't killed because they were Jews, where people haven't starved, where tens of thousands of women weren't raped, where people who are pianists don't have to learn 350 folk songs every semester." In this moment, I suddenly saw myself free: "Enough! This is what my father has wanted to do ever since the 1930s! Let's get away from here as fast as possible."

Maca looked at me rather sadly. "Yes," she said, "I'll come with you!"

"But how?" I stuttered. I did not know the answer to this question. At this point it was impossible to get a passport in Hungary to go anywhere and impossible to cross the border toward the West, not only because the border was constantly watched but also because there were mines in the crossings between Hungary and Austria. And the rest of the neighboring countries were just like Hungary, occupied by Russians—except for Yugoslavia, under Tito's rule. Tito, of course, resisted Stalin; nonetheless, one could be arrested there for other reasons. Indeed all of us knew this: it was impossible to leave the country alive.

That night when Pista came home, I told him about the strange experience and insight I had had.

"Of course," he said, "You're right! Let's leave! But how?" And we spoke about my poor father, who had tried everything to get visas in 1938 and

1939. When he realized that he would fail, he tried to get one for me and one for Iván. But even these attempts were unsuccessful. "Well," Pista said, "maybe there'll be a day when we'll be able to leave. And to be honest," he paused, "I can't wait!"

Within a couple of days I memorized 350 folksongs with Maca. But Pista's statement became essential to my view of the future: one day we might be able to leave Hungary. For the time being, however, this did not seem possible and, according to our pessimist friends, it would not be possible for the next hundred years.

Thank goodness, they were wrong.

19

Voyage to the East

In 1954, Pista unexpectedly received an invitation from the Society of Astronomers in the Soviet Union. Every astronomer at the Budapest Observatory was invited to participate in this conference. There was to be an eclipse of the sun that best could be observed in Russia during that summer. Pista left town with the other astronomers from the Budapest Observatory. Their plane flew out at the end of June, and they returned to Hungary at the beginning of August. During this time all the contact I had with Pista was through letters, several of which "got lost" (that is, they were destroyed by the overseers of the Hungarian or Soviet mail service), although others were allowed to arrive. Those I received usually took fourteen or fifteen days to get to me—and sometimes as long as three weeks. Of course, in these letters Pista could not give any account of his personal experience: his meetings and discussions with others, his own observations of the press, his impressions of Soviet intellectual life, or of people's standard of living. Rather, he would tell of the breakfast he had that morning or the music he heard by chance on the radio. He knew that he was not supposed to write about any detail of the trip except what they ate, drank, or saw in the mountains. Nor could he talk about his discussions with his colleagues. Therefore, the facts I read about in his letters did not touch upon whom he met, what he experienced, or how he felt. This was not a surprise, but still quite frustrating. I also feared for his life in the Soviet Union, and I missed him so much. I could not wait for his return.

* * *

During the time that he was away, I lived my life as before: practicing, playing chamber music, and seeing friends. But during this time, a major family catastrophe occurred as well that shook us all deeply: Marika, Pista's sister, died in Kölesd at the age of twenty-four. A beautiful girl with auburn hair and large, dark brown eyes, she had been sickly since early childhood after a recurrent bout of tonsillitis. She had developed heart trouble, which became so dangerous that she had to be taken to a hospital in Budapest in the spring of 1954. My father arranged treatment for her there, where he had two or three friends who were heart specialists. She was treated for several weeks in the hospital and had been showing signs of improvement even before István left town. Hence by the end of the spring semester she had gone home to Kölesd, postponing her exams at the university to the fall. In July of 1954, feeling somewhat dizzy, she tried to lie down on a bed when she suddenly collapsed and died. Her desperate parents were willing to postpone the funeral for a couple of weeks until István returned from the Soviet Union. The problem was, however, that he couldn't return. The poor man did not even know that he was supposed to return since he had no knowledge of what had happened. We tried everything, but it was in vain. We could not notify him either by mail or by telephone. I could not even send him a telegram. The official excuse of the telephone operator was that Pista and his group were on a mountain in the Caucasus, where the telephones did not work. Nor was the post office "as fast as it should be." A few days later Marika's funeral took place in Kölesd; it was held without her brother.

Two or three weeks passed before István returned to Budapest with the rest of his colleagues. Upon hearing that Marika had died, he was disconsolate. He went to Kölesd for a couple of weeks, returning in deep sadness. Seeing his parents' grief, he was at a loss as to how to help them recover, nor did he know how he himself would be able to stand on his own two feet again. It was a long time before he understood that he must. Circumstances forced him to do so. He had to finish his dissertation; he had to take his last exams; and he had to go ahead with his life, planning his future. Slowly, he did it. But for the rest of his life he would talk about Marika and cry. He never got over her loss and tragic early death.

* * *

As for his experience in the Soviet Union, he emphasized that the most significant aspect of the trip was his acquaintanceship with a couple of very friendly and highly intelligent East German astronomers. As it turned out later, he was right! These astronomers he met in the Soviet Union were instrumental in finding him a job and a fellowship in Hamburg when he escaped from Hungary in 1956 and was waiting in Vienna for an offer from Germany.

20

New Circumstances

During the years of 1953 through 1956, even the pessimists had to acknowledge the enormous changes in the Soviet Union and in virtually every country of the Soviet bloc. On the one hand, the pressure and the menace still loomed large. But after Stalin's death in 1953, the terror started to loosen. It seemed that the arrests of innocent people were less frequent, and the series of show trials were of less importance to the government. Then suddenly it became obvious that the Communist prime minister, Rákosi, was losing power and that the political pressure the government had forced upon the people was less brutal than it had been, less overwhelming. The purges stopped, some peasants were allowed to leave the collective farms to which they had been forced to move, and the fear of massive population transfers with the Russians slowly abated. Communism as we had known it for the past several years became less threatening than it was under Stalin—in Eastern Europe as well as in the Soviet Union.

Indeed, Stalin died in 1953. Suddenly rebellious voices could be heard resounding from all corners of Hungary—first from writers and artists, and later from students and workers as well. We did not, of course, learn about this development through the Hungarian media, except the *Literary Journal* (*Irodalmi Ujság*), which became more and more outspoken. We listened mostly to the BBC and to the Voice of America, and we met friends and acquaintances in the streets, in shops, and in our workplaces; all of our discussions concerned these political shifts. Everywhere people were speaking about their attempts to understand and follow the events playing themselves out in the country. They tried to hear what was behind the voices on the radio and the text in the newspapers. With growing delight we realized that significant, even observable changes were taking place in

Hungary. There was no doubt: the country was changing, and so was its relationship to the Soviet leadership.

I was beside myself. Was a revolution possible? A real revolution that would shake off the terror in which we lived? Would we live in a country where one day justice would prevail? I asked these questions to Pista, my father, and everybody else whom I could speak to about this issue again and again.

To calm me down Pista, seriously considering these questions, said yes, but I could see that he was not sure. Neither was I. I just wished it were true but doubted that it could be, despite the loud optimism of the BBC and the Voice of America discussing the issue. After all, the Soviet Union had occupied Hungary, and for essential changes to occur, the Western world would have to stand up for the freedom of occupied Eastern Europe. This did not seem likely, however, and we had to admit that the West neither appeared to be ready nor willing to do that.

Back in July 1953, Rákosi had resigned. In his place came Ferenc Nagy, who could not improve the Hungarian economy, which was in tatters. In addition, Rákosi was still strong enough to weaken Nagy's position. Their bitter dispute ended with Nagy's resignation a couple of years later and his condemnation by the Communist Party.

Nonetheless, soon after his resignation the Writers' Association and the Petőfi Circle (two groups led by Hungarian artists and intellectuals) started to discuss the record of the Hungarian Communist Party. They referred to its bloody history, denouncing the crimes it had committed against the people of the country. Slackening its reins, the Party withdrew somewhat. But this was just the beginning of its decline; on October 23, 1956 a nationwide revolution rose up against the Hungarian Communist government. It started out as a student demonstration marching across Budapest, calling for the evacuation of all Soviet troops from Hungary. The demonstrators were detained. Nonetheless the revolution was continued by others. Fired upon by the security police, one student was shot and killed. The revolt spread and the government's troops were soon defeated. By the end of October, the fighting was almost over. The revolutionaries won. The Soviets withdrew. Even so, the victory of the Hungarian Revolution lasted for just a few days. On November 4, large Soviet forces invaded Budapest and some other parts of the country. Moving into the capital, they quelled the uprising of the revolutionary army. Mass arrests and mass denunciations followed the defeat. In the battles, seven hundred Soviet troops and between twenty-five hundred and three thousand Hungarians were killed, thirteen thousand wounded, and within a few months two hundred thousand people fled the country. The Soviet actions had alienated many Marxists in the Western world as well, leading the Communist Party to a large loss of membership.

* * *

Around the middle of November, just as the attack of the Soviet army against Budapest started to calm down, my friend Maca came to us on foot from Ujpest, a section which is part of Greater Budapest. Since the streetcars and buses were not functioning during and immediately after the revolution, she must have walked seven to eight miles. Bringing along some of her clothing, including a nightgown, a pullover, her toothbrush, and a comb, she told me that she had come to us because she wanted to leave Hungary, as did many thousands of people at this point. Hoping that we would want to leave too, she had come to leave with us rather than go alone. Indeed she had heard me talking about this. She knew that I wanted to leave right away, before the government could close the country's border again. There was nothing strange about this desire. At this point Hungarians were on the move. Our neighbors had left. Many of our friends and acquaintances from all over the city, from all over Hungary had left, too. The last we heard from them was perhaps a letter, sometimes a phone call bidding us farewell. My family and I had to acknowledge the seriousness of the danger. Since we were rapidly running out of time, we had to make the decision of when to leave. At least Maca was ready to do so.

My father met with some of his colleagues, listening as each worked out various routes that they planned to use for their own departures. Pista's colleagues also wanted to leave, and they, too, made one plan after another. A number of my classmates had left already. The urge to go drove every member of our family, especially Pista and me. Yet the naked fear for my parents and loved ones, which had seized me during the Holocaust and the bombardment of Budapest, returned and was more powerful than ever. In the chaos around us, I felt the horror intensely. "All through our life," I cried bitterly in Pista's arms, "my fear has never changed. We have never lived without humiliation, intimidation, injuries, and the fear of death. Never."

Pista felt threatened as well. He was yearning for a world in which he could freely dedicate himself to studying mathematics rather than running from violence and the Communist Party's humiliating orders and demands for obedience. I reminded him again that there were lucky people in other parts of the world who could live with their heads held up high, such as

Éva Wimmer and her mother in Switzerland, my friend Marika Weiss in the USA, Marica Marko in Australia, and others scattered elsewhere. I felt intensely that we had paid our dues, and I wanted nothing else but to live free from fear and menace. My father, who had desperately and unsuccessfully tried to leave Hungary during the early 1930s when he recognized the danger waiting for us, now started to hope for what he heretofore had never achieved: to leave Hungary and live a life without shame and humiliation, without poverty and the fear of poverty, a life in which he was not constantly frightened by brutality and murder. He, too, started to make plans for departure. Although he was aware of the difficulties he might run into as a fifty-eight-year-old man arriving in a foreign country without money, support, or relatives, his strength and ingenuity gave him confidence.

The border was still open in the beginning of November 1956. Iván came along to Budapest from Pusztamonostor, the small town where he lived, accompanied by his wife Mari, who was eight months pregnant. They came to tell us of their decision to leave the country with us. There seemed to be no reason to stay in Hungary. In fact, large numbers of young people had already left. Most were in professions they felt they could use elsewhere, or they hoped for new job opportunities or new areas of study. Finally, my mother agreed to leave, too.

But shortly after Iván and Mari arrived, bad news started to sweep over Budapest. The BBC and the Voice of America reported casualties on the border. In addition, several of our closest friends felt that their task was to tell us not to go. Some of them directly wrote or called to recommend that we reconsider our plans.

"Leaving is dangerous," our former neighbor said, who had tried to leave but returned from the border. "A lot of people have been arrested. Obviously some will be taken to Russia; some will lose everything in the end. Don't risk it! Don't go!"

Indeed, people who were arrested for trying to cross the border and were denounced by their neighbors or the caretakers of the houses in which they had lived had their apartments taken from them right away, with all of their belongings. Panic broke out. Suddenly there were mass arrests at the border. Many people reconsidered their decision. My parents started to hesitate.

"Unless we find a way of crossing the border that is 100 percent secure, we can't go," my mother cried. "I don't want to be imprisoned, nor do I want to lose everything!"

My father agreed with her and so did my brother. At this moment, we moved into the air shelter because shots swept over the streets again. And as I sat on a chair covered by a grey-blue blanket in the basement of our house, just as I had done twelve years before in the basement of a house in Kisfaludi Street, where we hid during the Siege of Budapest, I realized that these talks were taking us nowhere. Suddenly it became obvious to me that all this was nonsense. We would never find a 100 percent secure way to flee. We had to risk our security if we wanted to leave. And while the Soviet troops attacked the city and artillery shells exploded everywhere above and around us, I could do nothing but beg my father again and again:

"Please, reconsider! Let's not stay here any longer! We're persecuted here! We are always hungry and always afraid! We have had enough bombs falling near us! Let's go, please, let's go!"

And when the cannon fire and shooting stopped, and we moved from the shelter back into our apartment, I lay at night as close to Pista as possible, crying.

"We must leave! We can't tremble all our lives fearing the Nazis, the Communists, the war, everything! We must leave! I don't want to spend my life and your life and our future children's lives in the shelter trembling from the falling bombs. We can't stay here." I sobbed, "We'll always be afraid," adding, "I was always afraid! All my life, I was always afraid!"

Pressing my body to his, he said, "I know. If we stay, we'd be living the life of the dead here, and then one day we'd die anyway."

This was an unusually sad and cynical statement coming from Pista. I suddenly had the feeling that he had become skeptical and had lost the drive to escape that he once had. He had grown tired, and I knew why. The news about leaving started to become terrifying not only because people had been caught and taken to jail but also because the arrival of tens of thousands of refugees in Vienna often did not bring the result the refugees had been expecting. After crossing the border, some of our friends and acquaintances wrote to us about the frustration and misery of waiting in front of various embassies to speak to high-level officials, hoping to ask for help in finding a country that would take them in. Others called us from Vienna (remarkably enough, the telephones worked throughout the revolution and after its collapse as well) to tell us about the long lines of people waiting for days and then weeks in front of various embassies, only to learn that they could not go to the country they hoped would accept them. They wrote about the terrible dangers they faced on their long walks to cross the border. Some lay on the ground for days in man-made holes covered by leaves while the Russian soldiers searched for refugees. Others were a whole week in the forest, hidden behind the trees without food and warm clothing because the Hungarian guards were looking everywhere for them.

Yet I worked it out quite clearly for myself: leaving was dangerous, but staying was even more so. There was nothing more dangerous than a city under siege or a country ruled by terror. What should we do? Obsessed by fear for my father's life and Pista's, I wanted us to leave together. The rest of my family, however, had by now (during and after the second half of November) too many questions about the new dangers of crossing the border as well as what life would be after our arrival in a new country. Iván knew that in America he would have to retake all his major medical exams, a project that would take years to complete, and he did not seem happy to have to take them again. Also, he and his wife spoke no English. How long would it take him to learn the language well enough to take the exams? And what about their baby? Somebody had to work. Who would be the breadwinner? Then there were some desperate matters that my father started to discuss. True, he was an excellent businessman and had made many discoveries in the field of medicine. But he did not speak English well, and he had no friends or relatives in any other countries but Hungary. As for me, I was not worried. I knew that nowhere in the Western world had people been forced to live in ways we had been in Hungary for the past decades. I wanted to live in peace without the threat of the yellow star, without exploding bombs, without the fear of deportation, without constant hunger. I also wanted an apartment with a functioning bathroom, and I hoped that sometime in the future I would have nice dresses to wear. In addition, I hoped that if one day we had children, they would not have to live under the pressure and fear that we had all our lives. If we could finally live in peace, I thought, I could deal with any difficulties that we might initially face in a foreign country.

What Pista wanted was simple. First of all he, too, wanted us to feel free. He wanted to be left alone to study mathematics and live without the ever-present pressure and intimidation from the Party.

He agreed with me unequivocally and kept on repeating, "You're right, of course! We must go! But the question is how?"

It was the end of November 1956. Time was passing. We knew that we could not wait much longer, for the Soviets had won and the border would not stay open forever, even half-open. We were also aware of the fact that it was less dangerous to go now than it would be a week or two later. We had a few opportunities for fleeing offered to us, but none of them seemed secure enough to my parents; therefore, we missed all of them. We dared not leave. After spending several days in our apartment and making new plans every minute, Maca abandoned the idea of leaving Hungary with us. She walked home to her mother and never tried to flee again.

But Pista and I didn't give up our hope. We talked about it every moment we were together. He decided to go to Kölesd and tell his parents that he wanted to leave; he came back to Budapest with their blessing. In fact, he told me how selfless they were: they thought of him rather than of themselves, begging him to go. "You must go! You can't stay here! If you do, your life will be ruined!"

But we didn't know what to do, where to turn, or whom to talk to. Despite the fact that many people were being caught at the border, thousands were leaving daily. Time passed.

One day at the end of November, the parents of Károly Balogh, an astronomy student with a scholarship at the observatory, arrived in Budapest to visit their son. They came to tell him that they would be happy to take him and his family either back to Sopron, the town where they lived (on the western border of Hungary, next to the Austrian border) or, if Károly and his family wanted to leave the country, across the border. It was still possible to go to Austria. In fact almost all refugees leaving Hungary went that way, walking across the country's western border. Upon arrival in Austria, they would then wait in Vienna for visas from the countries to which they had applied. At this point most of the mines between Hungary and Austria, which had been placed by the guards years before the revolution, were cleared out. So it appeared that while one still had to fear the guards at the border, there were no longer any mines underground. Still, to make sure that no harm would come to anyone, the Balogh parents offered to walk across the Austrian border with their son and his family—and with anyone else who wanted to join them. They said they knew where to go and where not to. They really did. Karcsi Balogh came down from the mountain to see Pista. He told him the news and offered both of us a place in their group if we wanted to leave with them. He did not have to wait long for our response; after a thirty minute discussion, he returned to the mountain to report our answer.

"You must go!" I held Pista's hand and kissed it again and again. "We won't have other opportunities! And even if we do, none will be as good as this one! And we'll never go if you don't go! We'll always just talk about it and never go! Ever! So you must go! You have no choice. I have no choice. We have no choice. And believe me! If you go, we'll follow you! My parents won't let me follow you alone. I am sure they'll come along. Don't be afraid. We will come! We'll come as soon as possible! Unless we want to live forever in this Hungarian misery, in this Hungarian horror, we'll go. We must! Enough! We must break the ice. I can't leave my parents. I don't have the strength to do that. It is you who must leave! If you do, my parents will follow along with me. But to make it possible for all of us to leave, you have to start!"

He knew that I was right. Taking me in his arms, he rocked me and kissed me for hours. Lying in bed as close as possible, we wept, our tears flowing together. I still feel their taste.

"No! I am not leaving without you," he said again and again.

"But you must," I whispered. "Otherwise we'll never go. We'll sit here for another fifty years, and all of this will go on endlessly. You must leave! Father has shown that while he wants to leave, he just can't. How much hunger, how much intimidation, how much fear will we have to go through over the years to come? How much humiliation, hunger, and poverty will we have to suffer? And how much fear, if you don't start? Haven't we had enough? Hasn't it been enough?"

Both of us knew that it was time for us to get away from Hungary. We had suffered for years, and our parents had suffered even longer. First we were Jews, then we were capitalists. First Pista's parents were peasants, then they were kulaks. To get away from our predictable future in Hungary, we both understood that István needed to leave and that his departure would involve our parting from one another. Clearly my parents could not face a walk across the border amidst the danger that threatened all of us, nor would they ever want to leave without my brother Iván. On the other hand, they could not bear the thought of my going off on this long walk with people they did not know, with Hungarian and Russian soldiers in the forests hunting for desperate escapees. They would not want me to leave with Pista on my own. They trembled at the mere thought of our walking across the border. Hence I felt that if any one of us could leave, it was Pista who would have the courage to do so. And if he went, nobody could keep me from going after him. I felt that there was no other solution: he must be the first to go. And all of this meant that we had a very short time in which to decide our future.

Two days passed. Then Karcsi called Pista, telling him that he and his family would leave town the next day, and if Pista wanted to come along he could do so early in the morning. Karcsi would come down from the mountain to pick him up. During the night we held one another closer than ever, shaking like dry leaves on the trees during a fall storm. We got up early in the morning and had breakfast: we knew that we would be parting for a long time.

One thought loomed large in my mind. "Maybe it'll be years." My hands shook when I thought again, "Maybe forever..."

When Karcsi rang the doorbell, I knew that I must not sob. I must laugh because we were starting to leave Hungary! István embraced me; my parents cried in the hallway. We said goodbye to him. Then he left. Standing on the balcony, I waved for a while. I was relieved and at the same time devastated.

21

Across the Border

Pista told me later that after he left with Karcsi, they went quite aimlessly in circles before going back to the mountain to pick up the rest of Karcsi's family along with Tibor and Pista Vidéki, a young man who worked in the observatory's workshop and who wanted to go along with them. Leaving Budapest, the group got on the train to Sopron with thousands of other refugees who filled every seat and stood in groups, taking every bit of space on the train. Standing meant being crammed together with the massive crowd of people that had pushed themselves onto the train. They were virtually unable to move their bodies for the next ten hours until the train arrived in Sopron. The usual travel time from Budapest to Sopron was three to four hours, the two cities being about 160 miles apart, but on this day thousands of people were still streaming to the border, most of them taking the train. Of course, some did go by car, bicycle, or carriage while others started on foot, hoping for the strength it would take to walk to the border and get out of the country. The train moved very slowly, stuck for hours at various stations, stopping again and again. It took from early morning to the evening for Pista and his friends finally to arrive in Sopron.

In the countryside, after a bite to eat in the little house of the Baloghs, the small group of young astronomers fell asleep. The next day in the early afternoon, István, Tibor, and Pista Vidéki set out with Mr. Balogh to cross the border into Austria. The momentous escape from Hungary occurred as uneventfully as possible.

As Pista told me four months later in Hamburg, "We walked lightly, slowly, almost imperceptibly for about thirty minutes and then we were in Austria. I looked around: we were *free*."

* * *

The two Istváns and Tibor found a place to sleep provided for Hungarian refugees arriving at the Austrian border. They had ten dollars between them for train tickets to Vienna, but they did not have to use it. Their money was not accepted at the ticket office of the train station when the employees learned that the three young men had come from Hungary. The Hungarian Revolution was highly regarded in most Western countries as an indication of resistance to the Soviet Union and its possible collapse. Escapees were being celebrated as heroes. In this case people bought lunch for Pista and his colleagues, and everything else they needed, including tickets for the train. Clearly Austrians recognized that they were exceptionally lucky to have become free of the Soviet presence in 1955. At the end of World War II, like all Russian-occupied countries, they had experienced the brutality of the Soviet military, which included cruel sexual violence against women and the complete plunder of the population by rank and file. And after the Russians had left Austria in 1955, people were obviously worried about the growing terror, poverty, and danger this occupation was creating in countries next to theirs. They feared the Russians' return. Hence the Austrians looked upon the Hungarian Revolution as the beginning of the end of Soviet rule. They celebrated this revolution and helped the fleeing Hungarians as much as they could.

22

New Life

The trip from the border to Vienna took Tibor and the two Pistas two and a half hours. Arriving in the capital, they left the station and caught a streetcar, which took them to the observatory. As soon as the conductor in the streetcar found out who they were, a similar process played itself out regarding the young men's wish to purchase tickets with their ten dollars. Neither the conductor nor the other passengers in the streetcar allowed them to pay.

Arriving at the observatory with letters of recommendation from the Hungarian Observatory's director, Detre, they were received with open arms by the director of the Viennese Observatory and the rest of the members of his institution. Less than forty-eight hours after his departure from home, Pista called me from Vienna.

Sobbing on the telephone, we celebrated. At the same time I assured him in the Aesopian language that we created for this purpose that I would follow him with my parents as soon as possible.

* * *

The next day, Pista wrote to the East German colleagues he had met in Russia two and a half years before; these kind people had offered him their help if he ever needed anything. At this point he told them that he had left Hungary and was in Vienna looking for a job and a fellowship at a university. Within a few days he received several fellowship offers combined with job offers from a variety of observatories. He chose Hamburg, Germany. Through the connections he had made at the conference in Russia, Tibor also got a job in Germany. Pista called me to say that he would have to wait for a while before he could receive a refugee visa to enter Germany. There was a bureaucratic process that had to be gone through before he could stay in Germany as a PhD student while becoming an assistant in the Hamburg Observatory.

"This is the best observatory in Germany," he told me, "and one of the best in Europe. I am happy to go there."

"And what about an assistantship in a math department?" I asked.

"That's not possible right now," he said. "I am prepared for my PhD exam, I have started my dissertation, and both are in astronomy. Later I can think about other possibilities."

"Is that right?" I asked.

"At this moment? Absolutely," was his answer.

"He must know what's right," I told myself. I was happy but at the same time deeply surprised. Going to Germany was a decision I had never considered before. I could easily have imagined going somewhere else in Europe or the United States, a place which had always been my father's dream, and I would have been very happy had we gone there. But Germany was a country I had never considered; it was a thought I had never been thinking about. On the one hand, German was my second mother tongue, but having lived through the Holocaust and having such deep, personal knowledge of "that what happened," I just could not imagine myself living in this country. Even so, I completely identified with German culture. I had grown up in it—as had my mother and grandmother, whose parents probably came from a Prussian background, from somewhere in the Pale of Settlement, and for whom speaking German at home was probably more natural than speaking any other language. Also, I had lived my life surrounded by German culture: my mother spoke to me in German and read me German books, starting with the Grimm's Fairy Tales and, as I got older, the major German children's novels. In addition, she sang and taught me German folk songs as well as a large selection of songs by Bach, Beethoven, Schubert, and Schumann. Besides Hungarian and Hebrew, my third prayer every night was in German: "*Müde bin ich, geh' zur Ruh . . .*" ("I am tired, go to bed . . .") And even when I was only four or five years old, she read to me some of the most beautiful Goethe and Schiller poems. We also had German nannies for a while. My mother hoped we would speak German as well as we spoke Hungarian.

But at this precise moment, with the Holocaust in my immediate past, every minute of it was alive in me as if it had taken place the day before. Every brother and sister of my parents had been killed at Auschwitz—except my father's brother who had been murdered by the Hungarian army as a Jew on the Russian front. While we were hiding and running for our lives for ten long months during the German occupation, we managed to stay alive only because our Erzsi saved the four of us and because the Russians liberated Budapest before we could be found and killed by the Hungarian Nazis. Still, having survived the extermination of six million Jews, we never contemplated living in Germany. Could we live there at this point? What would happen if they saw that I was Jewish? I knew nothing about the world there, nothing about the new Germany. I only knew what had happened in the past. I spoke on the telephone as if I was thinking only about Pista's future. I could not say that I would be there, too. The state was tapping the phones again, and Pista was careful when talking.

"It'll be okay," he said. "I have a good scholarship and a good job as an assistant in the Hamburg Observatory. It'll be fine. In a few years I'll have my doctorate and a job at some university. It'll be wonderful!"

We did not talk about anything else. I was wondering, "Will it really be wonderful? And if somebody sees that I am Jewish, what then? How will I be able to make friends? What will I do there?" But I didn't say a word. I just listened to him. Lying in bed alone at night, I asked myself again and again, "How will it be? What will happen if I meet somebody who says that he was in the army during the war? That he killed Jews during the occupation? What will I say? And what will I feel?"

23

Waiting for a Miracle

Still, despite all my concerns I was driven by one desire only: to convince my parents of the urgency of leaving Hungary. But soon I had to admit that I could not do it. They were frightened and totally unready. They became increasingly afraid of being caught at the border by Hungarian or Russian guards in the middle of winter (it was by now December 1956).

"It's too late. We should have fled in the 1930s. Now it's dangerous. In the forest alone in no man's land, we'll lose our way, and the guards will find us," said my father while my mother could only cry.

Indeed, by the beginning of December 1956 Hungarian soldiers were back at the border crossings, and if they discovered who we were, they would indeed arrest and bring us back to Budapest. In the meantime we would lose all of our belongings, including the library, my father's last cello and last violin, my Steinway, and our apartment. We did not know whether we would be arrested and sentenced for years as some escapees had been or just set free, but that we would be homeless forever we knew for sure. The border had been open for more than six weeks, but now it was closed, and those caught crossing it were in jail.

However painful it was to think about this, I knew that my parents were afraid of making this decision. They would not only have to leave my brother behind but also run the risk of incarceration and the loss of everything we still had after the Holocaust, including our beautiful apartment, none of which could ever be replaced in Communist Hungary. Caught at the border, we would become homeless, the thing I had feared most all of my life. Of course, many people were still leaving—sometimes several hundred, sometimes several thousand a day. Many were caught and brought back to Budapest, yet most managed to arrive in Austria. It was just a matter of luck who got through and who did not.

December passed, and so did January.

For the first time in the last few years, I did not practice six to eight hours a day; rather, I was preoccupied with talking to people about leaving. A couple of my friends, with the help of their acquaintances, brought me into the company of others who also wanted to flee and people who were ready to smuggle anybody across the border—for big money, of course. These friends of mine knew someone who said he would take me across the border to Austria with nine others. He would do this for three hundred dollars, a huge sum of money in 1957 Budapest, especially for Hungarians, whose poverty was even more pitiful than before the time of the mass flight. This man, like the parents of Karcsi Balogh, came from one of the towns located a couple of miles from the border region. I was told that he would pick me up from his friend's house and take me to Austria with others who wanted to come along. With Pista in Hamburg and my own determination to leave Hungary, I knew that I must decide by myself what to do. This I did. I said farewell to my parents and in terrible distress and anxiety, left them behind. We were a company of nine people who travelled together with our "leader," whose house was placed in the town of Győr, close to the border.

But my father followed me incognito, going behind our group from the East Train Station in Budapest to our leader's home in Győr, from which we planned to set out early in the morning. I slept on the floor in my winter coat and left the house next day with the rest of the group for our walk across the Austro-Hungarian border. It was a cold, gray, rainy, snowy winter day, and as we set out I suddenly caught a glimpse of my father standing on the other side of the road. Realizing that it was actually him whom I was seeing, I found myself unable to breathe or even move. I felt powerless to go on. I could not leave him, nor did I feel able to continue walking with the group across town and then across the border. I was paralyzed with fright. I wanted nothing more than to weep in his embrace.

I stepped away from the group. Our leader wanted me to step back and immediately join the rest. But I told him that I had reconsidered: I could not go and leave my life behind. He screamed at me something about the necessity of knowing what one wants to do, but the choice was not his to make. I was determined to stay. My father stood in front of a house, pretending to read a poster glued to a tree. Waiting until the group left, I ran across the street and fell into his arms. He sobbed, apologizing for having followed me. We turned back and went to the station, where my father bought our tickets to Budapest.

The next day I had returned to the chaos I had wanted so desperately to leave for so long. I knew that I must keep on fighting and that I must find someone I could trust. It also had to be someone my father could trust, a person who would take me across the border. A week after my unsuccessful attempt to leave, I got on a streetcar and went to Pest, where I met a friend of mine in a café. After our meeting, I was about to leave when I came across an acquaintance, a kind violin teacher at the Béla Bartók School of Music. I had played chamber music with some of her students. I sat down and talked with her for quite a while, telling her about Pista and about my hope of finding someone to take me across the border.

"I know such a person—at least I think I do," she said, adding, "but I believe it will be very expensive." Then she mentioned the name of a conductor whom I had met years before during the intermission at a concert.

During the Communist era most people did not make enough money by working just one job. Those who could find a second one ate better and lived better. Nonetheless I was shocked when I heard that a musician, a conductor would smuggle others out of the country for money. This I would never have imagined. But apparently I was wrong. The musician in question did precisely that. He obviously needed the extra income. And that was my luck.

The next morning, my father and I met with him. He told us point blank that he needed four hundred dollars to bribe a number of people who would be part of the process of getting me a passport. Well, four hundred dollars was an incredibly large sum of money in Budapest in January 1957. At that time tens of thousands of people were still trying to run away from the country, often not having enough time to sell expensive musical instruments, furniture, and other goods, leaving them sometimes in the streets, sometimes in their own apartments. Nothing had a price; the American dollar was the only currency with any value.

It took weeks for my father to get four hundred dollars together. He borrowed from Iván, from friends, and from strangers. Some demanded incredibly high interest on the principal. But in the end, he put together the four hundred dollars needed by selling his Italian cello, my six-foot Steinway, and several of our beautiful paintings, which had survived in our apartment during the Siege of Budapest and the Holocaust. With Erzsi moving into our apartment, her presence had saved everything we owned. Of course, after the war, during the starvation period in Budapest, my father had had to sell some of our beautiful Persian rugs to be able to buy us food. But we still had kept his cello, my piano, and the paintings. At this point, however, he sold everything that was left to get together four hundred dollars. Eventually he paid the conductor, who then made arrangements for my passport, which I received within a few weeks.

On the sixteenth of March, the conductor and I left for Vienna. As long as I live, I will not forget the moment when I said farewell to my parents. My heart broke, and it has not healed since. Yet I left. Going to the station with my father and kissing him for the last time as we were standing at the platform, I felt a pain in my chest sharper than any I have felt in my life. Raising my head high, I swallowed back my tears and got on the train with the conductor.

Shortly after the train started, the conductor asked me to keep his handkerchief in my winter coat's pocket because he had no room to keep it anywhere: all of his pockets were full. "Of course," I answered, and he put his handkerchief very carefully into my winter coat's pocket. At the border the Hungarian military carried out a detailed search of the travellers. Guarding the border, they were looking for jewelry, gold, and foreign money. After a while, however, they stopped the search; they found nothing. Leaving our compartment, the men withdrew. After a while, standing outside our compartment at the window, the conductor asked me to give him back the handkerchief. "May I?" he asked me.

"Of course," I answered, letting him reach into the pocket of my winter coat. He did so, taking out his handkerchief very carefully and opening it in front of me: wrapped in its middle was a huge diamond ring.

* * *

Tibor was waiting for me at the station to take me to the observatory. I was invited to stay there until I received my West German visa, which István had arranged for me in Hamburg. I went with Tibor to the German embassy, where I had been promised I would not have to wait very long. Indeed, it took only one week for me to receive my German visa so I could leave Vienna for Hamburg. István met me at the train station and we took the train together to Bergedorf, where the observatory was located. I could not stop sobbing. Around us sat some surprised and worried Germans. At first they must have thought they were witnessing some family drama, but later one offered me a handkerchief, and another, water. I knew I should stop crying, but I could not. Burying my head in Pista's lap, I cried during the whole trip from Hamburg to Bergedorf—and so did he.

In Bergedorf we walked from the train station to the observatory. As soon as we arrived there I tried to call my parents but could not get through. It took several hours before the Hungarian telephone center answered and was able—and willing—to connect us. Despite the fact that I made the connection in the evening around 5:30 P.M.—, it was 2:00 A.M.—when I could finally talk with them. The next day my father said he would go to Kölesd to tell Pista's parents that both of us were safe and well.

24

Hamburg

The first person I met after my arrival at the observatory was Dr. Dickvoss, one of Pista's supervisors. I entered the office, and after introductions Dr. Dickvoss took me to the kitchen and asked me to make some tea for the three of us. After a minute alone in the kitchen, I called for Pista, pretending that I needed some dishes from the shelf.

When he came in I whispered, "How do I make tea?"

He simply and clearly told me in Hungarian what was essential for this not too terribly complicated process: "Boil water, put a spoonful of tea leaves in the teapot, and pour the boiling water over them."

Of course, we could not say in front of Dr. Dickvoss that I had never made tea in my life. Both of us felt we had better not speak about this

Figure 10. Zsuzsi and her father in Berlin (1958).

particular problem of mine. Five minutes later I produced a pot of tea, my first ever, and I felt pride and shame alike.

Indeed, later that night I told Pista that I was terribly ashamed of myself, letting my mother do everything around the house by herself. In fact I had never helped her do anything. He, too, said he was ashamed that he had never helped either. We had let her shop by herself, carrying heavy bags filled with potatoes, vegetables, and other food to Rózsadomb (Rosehill), where we lived. We had let her clean, cook, and bake. She had also prepared tea or coffee for us several times a day, and we had left her alone with all these chores, expecting her to do everything. Too late we faced up to our neglect. We lay in bed in Hamburg-Bergedorf as we first discussed this shameful issue. In vain I cried bitterly. What had happened in the past could not be changed. Those years after the war could not be erased; they would remain part of our lives for as long as we lived. Now, however, we knew that we had to change. And I saw clearly that István was right when he said that both of us must learn how to do everything because there was nobody now who would help, nobody who would provide for us.

25

First Steps

Indeed we had much to do in Hamburg after my arrival. Pista's life had already been settled to some extent: he enrolled as a PhD student at the university and had a job as an assistant at the observatory in Hamburg-Bergedorf, where he was expected to work for six to eight hours a day, evaluating the work of a several astronomers who were observing a group of stars. While he was not obliged to take more classes, he had to complete his dissertation with Professors Dickvoss, Heckmann, and Wachmann on his committee.

My tasks were arranged shortly after my arrival. First I, too, received a German "refugee passport," which assured me of the rights of an asylum-seeking foreigner in Germany and gave me the opportunity to travel and live practically as a citizen of the country. And I could apply for citizenship later.

As far as my piano studies were concerned, I played at a rehearsal of the Hamburg Academy of Music and was accepted into the concert pianist program, becoming a student of Eduard Erdmann, the famous German pianist. I also received a scholarship. What started out so fabulously did not work out, however. My studies with Erdmann did not last long. A year after my arrival, he died. My next teacher was Mademoiselle Zur, who was very helpful in preparing me for my concert diploma. By that time I was already uncertain as to whether I should pursue the very profession which had been my passion and my life's hope since childhood. These concerns were not new to me but, in Budapest, surrounded by my family and my own past as a pianist, I had felt unable to change my situation either psychologically or practically. In Hamburg I felt stronger and more independent, yet I still could not make a final decision. How could I give up what I had loved so much, the ideal and practice with which I had grown up, my soul's deepest desire all my life, the dream of my father?

Again Pista's opinion and help were instrumental in changing my thinking on this dilemma.

"You must do what you are most interested in," he said. "That should be your first goal. And don't forget, whatever you decide, I'll support you! Of course, I see and understand that you feel pressed to make a decision. But try to disregard this pressure. You have time! Just think about it: things change. And these changes, I believe, make our lives more interesting and more beautiful. Think about it, how boring the world would be if everything would remain the same. . . . Do whatever you think is the best! You'll have time to do it!" With his realistic approach and his appreciation of me and my own hopes, desires, and interest in the future, he helped me to make up my mind.

* * *

After a short while we found an apartment in Reinbeck near Bergedorf, but we were not allowed to use its kitchen or bathroom. Besides our small rented room, the only other place we could use in this apartment was a tiny bathroom that had no bathtub, just a washstand and a toilet. To keep myself clean I had to go to the observatory's public bathroom, where I was allowed to take a shower.

During my first few weeks in Germany I went every morning with Pista to the train station. He would take the train to Bergedorf, and from the station he would walk to the observatory. I, on the other hand, would travel to Hamburg, to the music academy. I had to go there because I had to practice, and since I did not have a piano in Reinbeck nor in Bergedorf, the only place for me to practice (not always, but most of the time) was the music academy itself. I would arrive there hoping to find an empty room where I could stay and practice for the next eight to ten hours. Sometimes I would find such a room; other times, I would not. Yet I always hoped to discover a miracle. Still, these were miserable times, which caused me terrible anxiety every day. I saw my career gradually falling apart.

But then a month or two after my arrival, I met Mrs. Schreiber. A colleague of Pista's, Kurt Eberlein, had a friend who taught at a school in Lohbrügge (a section of Bergedorf). This friend asked the school's caretaker Mr. Schreiber whether his friend, a pianist and student at the music academy, could practice in the school on weekday afternoons (at this time middle schools in Germany were in session daily until 1:00 P.M., and just once or twice a week until 2:00 P.M.).

Mr. Schreiber said, "Yes, of course! And during the weekends as well." So from spring 1957 until I received my diploma in the summer of 1961, I would arrive at the school where Mr. Schreiber worked between 1:30 and 2:00 P.M. and practice until late at night. In the meantime Mrs. Schreiber, who welcomed me with open arms, visited me in the music room several times in the afternoon as well as the evening, bringing me coffee and cake and often inviting me for supper. I usually left the school at 10:00 P.M. and took the train back to Reinbeck. Yet without the kindness of the Schreiber family I could not have received my concert diploma, nor could I have kept my sense of purpose alive. Their goodness, friendship, and appreciation of my work allowed me to practice every day, a routine which eventually made it possible for my life to become normal again. I started to stand on my own feet and believe in the future. I slowly overcame my concern and mortifying fear for my parents' survival and terrible pangs of conscience for having left them alone.

In addition to the love and help of the Schreibers, there was another family without whose continual help and support I could never have made it in Hamburg: the Wachmanns. Dr. Wachmann was one of the members of Pista's PhD committee. He lived with his wife and two children at the observatory in Bergedorf. Upon meeting me Mrs. Wachmann invited us for dinner, and when she heard that I was a pianist who had no piano and was allowed to practice in a middle school only in the afternoons and evenings, she offered me her house and her piano for use during the morning hours. Earning my concert diploma and being able to practice every day for ten hours or so was possible only with the help I received from these two kind and warm-hearted women who took a deep interest in me. They overwhelmed me with their love and motherly care.

I often talked with them about their pasts, about politics, about Hitler and the regime under which they had lived in their youth, learning much about their lives and those of others during the Third Reich. Mrs. Schreiber was the wife of an old-fashioned social democrat who had known the Nazis from the beginning. He and his father, with whom I had some interesting discussions throughout my stay in Hamburg, had been members of the Social Democratic Party since the early 1920s. For several generations most of their family had been workers at the harbor in Hamburg, as was the family of Mrs. Schreiber, whose members had lived in the city of Lübeck before the couple moved to Hamburg.

I got to know them and one day saw a photo of Mr. Schreiber as a young man, holding up a big sign that read: "*Wer Hitler wählt, wählt den Krieg*" ("Who votes for Hitler, votes for the war"). It was a sign that he had carried during several street demonstrations in the early 1930s. In 1938, I was told, he had been arrested and taken to Neuengamme, the concentration camp near Hamburg, where he lost three fingers on one of his hands.

Mrs. Wachmann originally came from a family of city dwellers, not overly interested in politics. Living through the Third Reich, she and her family were not directly affected by the regime, making every attempt to stay away from it as much as possible. But, of course, in the end they could not. Whole German cities were devastated by the bombing of the Allies, and no one could claim neutrality anymore. It was then that she came to understand what was happening around her. Deeply regretting the horrors committed under the system—facts she only later learned about—she told me in despair:

"Nobody asked me to think about it, nobody told me to look around and see what was actually happening! And I didn't know because my eyes were closed for a long time! I am so sorry, so sorry!" she cried in shame. At the same time, she did everything to feed me, love me, and care for me. Who was I to call her or our friends responsible for what had happened? They were not, and I loved them deeply!

* * *

Dr. Wachmann was also very kind to Pista, who worked day and night to finish his dissertation. And around us were a number of students and young researchers. All of them were young men, and all of them were outraged about what had happened in Nazi Germany. Some of them admitted that as young boys they had been excited and ardently dedicated members of the *Hitler-Jugend* (Hitler Youth), an association that promoted a "healthy" and "beautiful" life for German youth and a strong and victorious German future. Ashamed at having been deceived during the Nazi era, they now wanted to live free of the past and forget about the deceitful lies in which they had once believed. Incredulous and angry, each now felt the pressure of "that what happened" (Paul Celan's reference to his poem "Death Fugue" in an essay about Auschwitz). Yet some had been too young to do anything about it or even to know the details of the past for which they were feeling blame. Most had just started or not even been in middle school or high school during the time of Nazi rule.

One of Pista's colleagues was Engelbert Schücking, who had been in many ways different from other young German men: he came from an old noble family that had been social democrats ever since the beginning of the twentieth century. His father, who had been the mayor of Husum, resigned from his job in 1933. The family withdrew to their five hundred-year-old property at Sassenheim, and they desperately hoped for a democratic leadership after the war. At this point they were dissatisfied, however. They saw Adenauer's government as coming from the right wing, which did not create the political background they had hoped for after the collapse of Nazi Germany. In their view the Nazi government was guilty of murder and the new rulers of Germany were a dangerous threat to world peace.

To me it was exciting to discover that most young people whom we knew in the observatory and in the Music Academy hated the past and felt deeply ashamed about it, blaming their parents for not having resisted. Our new friends visited us in our apartment several times a week (after a while we moved to Bergedorf and lived in the main building of the observatory), discussing, listening, arguing, and despairing about the events that had taken place under Nazi rule in Germany. But they also worried about the political tensions of the present and what they saw as the "new threat" created by the Cold War.

* * *

As for Pista, how did he feel? What was life in Hamburg like for him? At first it was difficult, because ever since he had decided to study astronomy in Hungary rather than mathematics, he had felt uncomfortable—not so unhappy that he was desperate but unhappy enough to regret his decision. Only when he saw hurtful political events taking place in the math or physics departments in Budapest did he say, "Actually, it's a good thing I'm not there anymore!" But at other times he was not happy with his choice in the observatory in Budapest or in Hamburg. In fact he was yearning to go back to mathematics.

My heart ached when I saw his conflict.

"How would I feel," I often wondered, "if I had to give up playing the piano?" At this point such an eventuality was not quite possible to me. I saw in his demeanor and heard in his voice that he was suffering.

"I am in the wrong field," he would often say, his face turning deeply sad.

"It's true," I thought each time we talked about it. But when we lived in Hungary, and he received his scholarship in astronomy, he was not able to reconsider and leave the observatory. In Vienna he could have decided to change his field and apply for a fellowship in the mathematics department. But by then how would his mentors, each of them an internationally well-known astronomer, feel about his decision? They had written letters of recommendation for him to observatories all over Europe and the United States, and Pista had reacted to the first offer that arrived from Hamburg. He had accepted it: he came to Hamburg and felt that he had to stay and prove to everybody that he was worthy of the opportunities given him. He consoled himself with the thought that he was just working in astronomy for the time being, but he told me that later he hoped to study mathematics—as soon as he could. Of course, I saw that he was unhappy, but I could not say that he had made the wrong decision. Yet I feared that he might not be able to deal with the pressure, since he could not pretend or act differently from how he felt. He simply could not hide his disappointment: it was written on his face and affected his mood.

I feared that others might notice this as well. He carried a deeply felt honesty within himself, which had come perhaps from his childhood in Kölesd. It was a trait that stayed with him all his life. For this reason it seemed impossible to me that he would be able to carry on holding these jobs for any length of time. I tried to console both of us, wanting to believe that he would finish his dissertation within two or three years, and afterward he'd be able to free himself. Then I thought or at least hoped he would be able to do whatever he wanted. We were both so naïve! We did not ask how he would stand the pressure until then. Nor did we ask whether he, being employed somewhere as an astronomer, would be able to teach and research in any other field than astronomy. In fact we both thought and hoped that he would get a doctorate in astronomy, get a job at a university, and be able to turn back to his studies in mathematics. Of course, no such university system exists. One is expected to work in the field in which one has been employed, whether it be the field of astronomy, German literature, biology, engineering, or any other in the sciences or the arts. But we did not know that. Neither of us had come from an academic background. For the moment I thought it best for him to avoid the "political pressures" at the university, which made it possible to deny almost everybody an academic job. Indeed, at this point in history the German universities did not offer jobs to so-called "foreigners"; in fact, the number of jobs offered by them at all was minimal. Of course, the outcomes of these pressures were not very acceptable for many young German scientists. Still, we told ourselves that we were well off because, in spite of everything, we did get away from communism and from the political pressure under which neither of us was capable of living.

It's true that Pista had avoided this pressure in Budapest as much as he could. He even had opportunities for wide-ranging contacts. When he visited Russia in 1954, he met all those astronomers at an international conference, who went on to help him in the winter of 1957 to get offers from observatories after he fled from Hungary and arrived in Vienna looking for a scholarship or a job to start his life anew. In fact, on arriving in Hamburg Pista had a job, a scholarship, the opportunity to earn a PhD, and with it a future in the Western world of science. If he could just stand the pressure for two more years, I kept saying, he would be able to finish his dissertation and accept a job somewhere in Germany, maybe even in Hamburg. Then he could start studying mathematics again and slowly change fields. Sometimes I thought he also believed this, but at others I feared he did not.

And yet in the end, he was right: he found the focus of his interest, the direct goal of all of his hopes. Indeed we were lucky, enormously lucky.

* * *

Working at the Hamburg Observatory, Pista began to talk about mathematics and theoretical physics with Engelbert Schücking, and after a while Engelbert became interested in Pista's ideas. The two young scientists began to work together on geometrical aspects of relativity and Einstein's field equations. Of course, Pista had first to complete his dissertation on astronomy, which he did in 1959, but what mattered to him now was the work he had done with Engelbert on the "Exact Solutions of Einstein's Field Equations."

In fact, they became interested in Albert Einstein's theory of gravitation and its relationship with the ideas of the German physicist and philosopher Ernst Mach. Pista told me that Mach proposed a principle stating that objects do not move relative to space, but only relative to one another. The British physicist Felix Pirani interpreted this philosophy explicitly as follows: "If space-time satisfies Einstein's equations without any mass, then it must be the 'empty,' uncurved Minkowski space-time which does so." Drawing upon their mathematical expertise, Pista and Schücking were the first two researchers to write down a solution to Einstein's equations that contains no mass but is distinct from "Minkowski space-time," thus violating Mach's principle as formulated by Pirani. Their paper, "An anti-Mach Metric," was published in 1962 and has been viewed by relativists as a landmark in what has since been called "the golden age of general relativity" (Kip Thorne, *Warping Spacetime: The Future of Theoretical Physics and Cosmology*, 2003). Of course, this was a turning point in Pista's career. Relativity became his intellectual passion: the fulfillment of his interests and dedication. Publishing a number of articles and book chapters in this field, he became an internationally known and a deeply honored scientist, working on this issue and on other aspects of relativity for the rest of his life.

Pista and Engelbert went by train weekly from Bergedorf to Hamburg to participate in the Jordan Seminar. The seminar was led by Pascual Jordan, the famous German theoretical physicist. Jordan was accused of Nazi collaboration after the war, and perhaps not completely without reason. For he was indeed an analyst at the rocket center in Peenemünde. But Jordan had also supported Jewish physicists during the Nazi period, and in the 1950s he regained his professorship at the University of Hamburg. The director of the Observatory at Bergedorf, Professor Heckmann, was also interested in the physical aspects of astronomy and even in some aspects of the new research being done by Pista and Engelbert. As a matter of fact, Heckmann generously allowed the two young men to work on problems in which they were interested rather than on the topics he initiated. In this way life again became exciting and fulfilling for Pista; the future promised a world in which he would be free to read and work on problems of mathematical physics that interested and inspired him deeply.

He started to enjoy both his professional life and the world of Hamburg. Regaining his sense of satisfaction in life; his happy outlook; his sweet, peaceful, and happy smile, he felt that he could look forward to a beautiful future and a life of fulfillment.

26

Crisis

But while Pista's life changed for the better, mine became more problematic. Collapsing under the pressure of both past and present, I felt my world faltering. Having abandoned my parents in Hungary, I was tormented by my perceived betrayal and started to collapse under the pressure of our separation.

We had survived the Holocaust. But the impact of the war on our life was immense. Even during the late 1930s, years before the German occupation of Hungary, my parents had been aware of the persecution and murder of Jews all over Europe. As a child I sometimes overheard bits and pieces of discussions among my parents and their friends, some of whom were refugees from other countries, whispering to one another about the anti-Jewish laws and the atrocities taking place in Austria and Germany. After March 1938, Austrian relatives of my parents' friends found refuge in Hungary, and after Poland was occupied in 1939, new groups arrived. Later, other people came from a number of different countries that were under German occupation. In this way my parents had heard about the threat Hitler posed from the beginning, including the boycotts and measures taken against the Jews. My father had tried to get passports and leave Hungary as fast as he could, but his attempts amounted to nothing. There were several reasons for his failure. In the early thirties my mother was unwilling to leave her home behind. A large part of our family, including her father, had a very good life in post-World War I Yugoslavia, and we went to see them for two months every summer. In fact neither my mother's sisters nor her brother even considered leaving the place where they lived. Neither had my father's family wanted to flee.

Later, when the Germans occupied Austria in 1938 and Poland in 1939, we heard more and more horror stories from refugees fleeing to Hungary about the treatment of the Jews by the Germans. As my mother listened to them, she started to declare herself ready to flee, but by that time it was no longer possible to do so. Even so, my father tried everything, and when he saw that the four of us could not leave together, he tried to save at least Iván and me. But even this plan did not work. No country would accept us; it was impossible to get away, together or separately. After a while I heard horror stories from friends and friends of friends regarding the atrocities to which the Austrian and Polish Jews had been exposed. Listening to them, I was terrified at the idea of being separated from my parents. Just thinking about it, I would tremble and have nightmares when I went to bed. In fact, my obsession before and after the German occupation of Hungary was the same:

"What will happen to my parents? What I am going to do if I get separated from them? What? My God, what?"

But the Germans did not occupy Hungary until March 1944. Although by the end of the 1930s their lives were heavily burdened by antisemitic laws, Hungarian Jews were neither ghettoized nor deported until late spring 1944.

They were exposed to specific mass murders, however. In the summer of 1941, the Hungarian foreign office identified and deported about twenty-two thousand so-called foreign Jews who had fled to Hungary during the late 1930s and early 1940s from other German-occupied European countries. They were shot into mass graves in the Ukraine. Also, in the winter of 1942 the Hungarian army shot about fifteen hundred Jews and two thousand Serbs into the Tisza and Danube rivers in the former Yugoslavia—a terrain which had been taken away from Hungary in 1919 but which was "returned" to the country by Hitler in 1942. In addition, in the winter of 1941 to 1942, the Hungarian army killed, tortured, starved, or let freeze to death forty-five thousand to forty-eight thousand Jewish labor servicemen on the Russian front. Apart from these mass murders, no general atrocities or mass deportations of Jews took place in the country before May 1944. After the German occupation (March 1944), however, every Jew in Hungary was obliged by law to wear the yellow star (April 5); between the end of April and the end of May, all Jews in the country (750,000 people) were ghettoized; and by the beginning of July, all Jews in the countryside (about 500,000 people) were deported to Auschwitz, where most of them were killed.

We were not deported though, because Horthy stopped these actions at the end of June 1944 after receiving a letter from Franklin Roosevelt. The American president wrote that if Horthy didn't intervene at that point, when the war ended he would be personally held responsible for the deportation of the Budapest Jews. That the Germans and their allies had lost the war was quite obvious by the end of June and beginning of July in 1944. On the Eastern front, the Russian army had already taken back large amounts of territory from the Germans, and the Western allies had arrived on June 6 in Normandy. The end of the war was near, and the winners were undoubtedly the Allies. So Horthy cancelled the deportation of the Budapest Jews. But on October 15, 1944, when he sued for armistice, a Hungarian National Socialist government took over. At this point another "method of killing" was applied: large numbers of Jews were marched toward Austria, and those who were unable to walk were shot into pits in the countryside. Later, during the fall of 1944, the Hungarian National Socialists as well as the military shot thousands of people in Budapest into the Danube River. Nonetheless, probably 100,000 to 150,000 Jews survived in the capital. Thanks to Erzsi, the four of us stayed alive. But except for four children on my father's side (one in Palestine, three in Hungary) and two on my mother's side (one a Jewish slave laborer, another the daughter of a Christian mother), every member of my parents' large families was deported to Auschwitz and killed. My father's beloved brother Pali, who had been raised by my father because of their mother's early death, was murdered by members of the Hungarian armed forces as a Jewish labor serviceman on the Russian front. He was an uncommonly kind, loving, and highly cultured thirty-two-year-old lawyer. Their sister Lulu and her husband, too, were taken to Auschwitz. Likewise, my mother's three sisters Annus, Ila, and Böske were deported to Auschwitz together with their husbands and killed. In addition, her brother Imre was murdered as well as Imre's son, my cousin Gyurika (George), an exceptionally intelligent, talented, and sweet thirteen-year-old boy who had had his bar mitzvah one week before the Germans occupied the country.

* * *

Although we stayed alive, my parents had not recovered from the murder of their brothers and sisters, nor from the years-long period of intimidation, persecution, humiliation, suffering, and fear for their own and their children's lives. Neither had I, who had been hearing about the fate of the Jews in Germany ever since I was four or five years old. And then after the war, I also learned of the threat the Soviets posed to us. I understood almost immediately after our "liberation" that while the danger of the Nazis who had threatened us for many years was gone, a new danger took its place with the arrival of the Russian army. Not only did their invading forces create a rule of terror, but soon afterward it became clear that the Communist Party, unleashed by the Soviets, was committing unimaginable cruelties. In fact this Party became the overseer and organizer of the new political world in Hungary, and its power grew ever tighter. In the late 1940s we did not know about the agreement between Stalin and the other Allies, with Stalin demanding the territories of Eastern and Middle Europe for the Soviet sphere of influence rather than following these countries' own choice: the creation of democratic institutions. In the end, the Soviet dictator enforced his will and carried out his plans. Hungary and almost every Eastern European country became part of the Russian interest zone, following the directions and political changes of the Soviet Union. Hence walking in Stalin's steps, the Hungarian Communist government arrested large numbers of people, who faced show trials, death sentences, or were imprisoned and tortured for many years.

Devastated after I left Hungary without my parents, I feared that I would never see them again. At the same time, especially at the beginning of my stay in Germany, I kept hoping for a better future for all of us. Periodically I believed that one day a miracle would happen—they would come, and we all would do what we love to do: my father would create a new serum lab in Germany, my mother would be happy and forget about the worries and pain of life in Hungary, Pista would be allowed to dedicate his entire life to mathematics, and I would become a concert pianist. I even hoped at times that I might be able to bring our parents from Hungary— and perhaps even my brother Iván and his family would join us, and we would no longer live in fear but in freedom. But after a year or two passed, and I could do nothing about our separation, I felt that I had to face facts: I had to understand that Hungary would not change, my parents would never get a passport, and my dreams and hopes were not based on reality. I would have to deal with the fact that despite our flight from Hungary, we were not living as freely in Germany as I thought we would.

First of all, Pista had not yet passed his PhD exam, and while he was preparing to do so, we had to realize that he probably would not get a job as an academician. At that time there were very few jobs and just a handful of foreigners who had associate or full professor status at German universities. In fact, whether foreigner or German, in order to make a living in the early 1960s most PhD students in math or physics went into various branches of industry, probably because of the scarcity of academic positions.

"So what is he going to do?" I wondered, knowing that Pista was not the sort of person who would easily find his way in the job market. Sweet and warmhearted as he was, his world was different from that of most people. He was happy only when left alone, only when he could think and lose himself in his thoughts, wandering in a mathematical universe where he would find "solutions" for problems about which he had been thinking. While his dissertation, as I understood, dealt with some concrete astronomical issues, lately he was studying mathematics and theoretical physics, examining some major problems in this field with Engelbert Schücking, who had just passed his PhD exam in physics at Hamburg University. He now had a job for two years at the observatory. To imagine that after Pista finished his dissertation, he would go and work in the industry was almost unfeasible. I feared he would fail and suffer tremendously. I worried about his future.

Neither had I yet earned my concert diploma. And worse, my hope of becoming a professional pianist had shrunk significantly. My technique was still not good enough, and despite many hours of daily practice I did not seem to be making decisive progress. I was thinking of changing my profession but then let myself be convinced by István to graduate first and decide about everything else later. Nonetheless I felt the ground slipping from under my feet. My parents were not around, and there was no hope of ever seeing them for any length of time. No matter how often they applied for a passport, the Communist state of Hungary repeatedly denied their applications. In the end my mother did receive one for a two-week visit to us in Hamburg, and my father got one for just one week in 1959. But his passport was for East Berlin alone, and we could of course go only to West Berlin, where he visited us daily (this was just before the Wall was created). He visited us for a few days a second time in Hamburg in 1962. In the meantime he applied every six weeks for a passport which would allow him to stay for several months, but he was refused again and again.

In addition, none of my old friends lived in Hamburg. I had nobody to talk to about the past or the present, my situation a mirror of the past. This time it was the liberation that followed the Hungarian Revolution of 1956 that separated me from my best friends. Julika lived in Switzerland, the Sebőks in Paris, Maca and Ottó in Budapest, and Katalin in America. I felt I had no ground to stand on, nothing to hold onto, and no one to talk to. A huge abyss separated me from our new German friends whose parents had never been confronted by the Holocaust, even though most of them had been wounded by the war. Whatever had happened to them was different from what had happened to us. Entire German families had not been wiped out as the Jews had been in Hungary. And most important, after the war, Germans who survived went on with their lives whereas Jews in Hungary had no present, no past, and no future. Desperate at this point, I had increasingly painful pangs of conscience for having left my parents at home alone. With their families brutally murdered, they could of course never become whole again. Iván lived in the countryside and had little time to visit them in Budapest or even to talk to them on the telephone. I felt that my departure had made certain they would never recover. I felt responsible for their loneliness, their suffering, and what I saw as their unavoidable early deaths.

I was unable to discuss this hopeless situation with Pista. He, too, had left his parents; he, too, lived in a state of shock, not knowing what he would do after he finished his dissertation and passed his PhD exam. Why had we come to Germany only to have similar anxieties as those we had had in Hungary and fears just like in the past? What was a realistic goal in Germany toward which we could work? I knew that Pista had also been thinking of our uncertain present and uncertain future, and the very fact that I felt lost and frightened made him even more insecure.

I saw my life slipping away from me. I thought that we had left our home to create a better life for ourselves, but instead we had fallen into a deep hole out of which there was no return. I also felt that besides Pista, I had lost everybody whom I loved and that now I would have to live without the career in music for which I had been preparing my whole life. I felt that I could not face my father's disappointment at giving up my career, a future he had anticipated and was more happy about than anything else in the world. I felt that I had come to the end of my life: I had killed my parents by leaving Hungary, and I had ruined Pista. I felt I had no choice; I considered suicide.

And what was Pista doing during my decline? He was at times desperate, at others unable to fathom or handle this challenge. He suppressed it and worked in his office longer hours than ever before, coming home at nine or ten at night, sometimes even later. Why couldn't I speak to him? After all, it was I who had wanted so desperately to leave Hungary. Indeed, despite his dislike of the Communist system, without my pressure and the panic overwhelming me he would never have decided to leave. With our feelings so overwhelming on many levels, he began to grow unsure of himself, as he always did when I was in trouble. He tried to hide his problems from me. He also knew, he told me later, that I was afraid and tortured by guilt because I had left our parents. He didn't think he could talk to me about it. We lived on, each convinced that we should hide our pain and sense of failure from the other. In fact, since receiving his PhD he had been preoccupied with his studies and with the complicated aspects of his new environment, in which he, too, now felt alienated, nor did he see clearly what he was going to do in the future. For the time being he had received a job offer for two more years at the Hamburg Observatory, and he threw himself single-mindedly into his studies, working with Engelbert day and night. Since he believed that he could not stop my pain, he thought it would be better to leave me alone so that I could think about my life and make the right decision. As he told me later, he consoled himself with the thought that after a while I would come to understand that it had been right for us to leave Hungary, that after a while my parents would be able to follow us, and that in the end everything would turn out to be as good as before or even better.

But the truth of the matter is that Pista had his own concerns: he, too, had left his parents behind. They were elderly and had no other children. At the same time, he knew that soon he would have to make huge decisions regarding his own professional life and try to understand his future possibilities if we were to stay in Germany. He, too, had to face for the first time in his life our insecure future. With this recognition, he felt that the ground was opening up under his feet. Sensing his insecurity and fear of the future, I withdrew more and more, and after a while we stopped communicating.

* * *

I went downhill pretty quickly. I lived for the weekly telephone conversation with my parents. Since Pista and I did not have a telephone and we could not afford one, we went every Saturday to an inn, whose owner, Frieda, we had known for many years. She allowed us to use her telephone after 10:00 P.M. to call my parents in Hungary. However, getting through by telephone from Germany to Hungary at that time was no easy enterprise: sometimes it took an hour, sometimes two, three, or even more hours. And when finally we managed to get through, we had to be very careful about what we said, because the Hungarian national telephone service listened to and sent off telephone discussions to the Hungarian Secret Service, policing messages between Hungarians and citizens from other countries. Under these circumstances it was frustrating and very difficult to communicate. But at least we heard each other's voices.

Tortured by these problems and by my fear of my father's death, I never ceased to worry about him. He had a heart attack in the course of these years, of which I was only told ten months after it took place, and I never spoke to anybody about my growing pangs of conscience. I sank deeper and deeper into the chaos my own pain and fears created and found it increasingly difficult to talk. Again and again I reproached myself for wanting to leave Hungary in the first place and now for wanting to withdraw from my own decision. I fought with myself constantly.

Pista and I were tired at night and went to sleep immediately. Nor was there time or opportunity to talk during the day: I was off to practice, and he was working all the time. When I came home I would be unable to speak without immediately bursting into tears. I did not want to burden him. But I did so, of course, with my constant despair.

The only things we talked about when our friends came to visit was the role Germany played in Europe and the growing power of the Soviet Union. Although I enjoyed our discussions and our friends' important arguments, again and again my depression widened and I felt lost in every moment. Although he was busy with his work, Pista noticed my despair, but he didn't know how to talk to me. I felt more and more estranged from the world and even him, consoling myself that when I died, he would find someone with whom he could have a happy life. Still, despite my silence and his concerns about me, he would make me breakfast every day. He would also try to cook our supper, which I usually would not eat. He would pick me up every day from the school where I practiced and constantly try to talk to me about "my problem," but he just did not know how to do it. Who would have? I could not tell him that I had to go back to Hungary or else my parents would die of heartache. Then after a while, he, too, became depressed. Turning ever more silent, he sometimes grasped the moment, telling me over and over:

"I know that you are hurting! Please, tell me what I can do for you! There's nothing I wouldn't do! Nothing!"

But I couldn't speak; my throat was blocked. I wanted to go back to Hungary, but I abhorred the life I would have to live there. I also knew that I must not force him to go back with me because it would ruin him; as a deserter he would never get a job in Hungarian academia. In the end they might lock both of us in jail. At the same time, I knew that our separation would eventually kill my father.

* * *

Then a miracle happened. A friend of mine who noticed my deep depression recommended that I talk to her friend and colleague Dr. Cohen, a psychiatrist whom she knew well.

"He would understand you," she said.

I went to him, and within a couple of months indeed Dr. Cohen performed magic. I regained my balance and recognized my failure of judgment. To come back to the world and to see it again as it was rather than in its distorted form shaped by my nightmares was truly liberating. In fact it took just a short while for me to be able to see reality. I understood that I could not go back to Hungary because they would put me in jail, and by the time they let me go I would have no chance of becoming a concert pianist or beginning a new field of academic research. As a matter of fact, I would not even be accepted as a student at any institution of higher learning in Hungary. I also understood that whether Pista would stay or leave with me, I would ruin him as well. Finally, I saw that both my father and mother had to keep on trying to come to Hamburg and that I needed to be grateful for having been able to leave Hungary rather than play the game of returning to a country that was instrumental in the murder of almost all of my family members, a country where we never had a chance for our future, a country where I would never have a job! Also, I understood that in reality, I needed to allow myself to turn again to my best friend—my husband, my supporter, and my lover for many years, Pista, whom I adored—rather than feel constant pangs of conscience for having left with him.

When Pista saw me regaining my sense of reality and returning to my deep love for him, he celebrated: "It's like meeting you for the first time! Like falling in love with you again, again, and again!" He was overwhelmed by my love for him. He, too, came back to life. As if we had awoken from a nightmare immersed in a sad, lonely, hopelessly dark and cold world, we started to recognize the warmth of the sun, the colors and beauty of the day, and learned to live again in constant joy and deep happiness.

* * *

In the meantime, I received my concert diploma. After the concert I gave, I went to ESSO, working as a secretary rather than continuing my profession as a concert pianist. The experience was overwhelming. I encountered a new world totally unknown to me before. I practiced only on Sundays; on weekdays I took a U-train every day from Bergedorf to Hamburg and back, working in the office of ESSO. I can't say I loved it, but it was a new life, and going home every night to Pista, seeing him, embracing, and loving him gave me great pleasure: I felt secure and happy.

27

Major Changes

In the fall of 1961, our friend Engelbert Schücking was invited to the United States to teach a graduate course on general relativity during the spring semester at Syracuse University. At the end of June, on his return to Hamburg, he sat down in the big, dark gray leather armchair in our apartment at the observatory and said:

"We should have one goal now, and one only: moving to America." He went on, "We live here under a several hundred-year-old, oppressive academic system, with no jobs and no future! It doesn't offer us anything! In fact, it suffocates us! Let's go to America!"

This was the era of Sputnik. The US government as well as the American scientific community was concerned about the Soviets' progress in the field of mathematical sciences and physics and about the possible outcomes of this development. Hundreds of American department heads went to Europe to recruit academics, pursuing both young scientists and great ones from older generations who had not come to America during the 1930s and had not fled under the pressures of World War II and the threat of the Holocaust as many Jews and non-Jews had. Many of these European scholars did not yet have secure jobs in Europe or as many opportunities for further scientific development as American universities could offer. At the same time, most institutions of higher learning in the United States played up these advantages. During the spring semester of 1962, Engelbert and István both received offers from the University of Texas at Austin, and in the fall of the same year we arrived in America.

It was hard to leave Hamburg, the city where we had learned to rediscover one another and where we made so many close friends during our six-year stay. Among them were Pista's colleagues Emil Schuster and Klaus Bichteler—the first an astronomer, the second a mathematician—and others, including the Schreibers, the Wachmanns, and the great musicians Juan Allende, Gerd Zacher, and their friends. Juan had been a composer and Gerd a wonderful organist who could also imitate famous entertainers, making fun of popular music in an incredibly comical fashion, the likes of which I have never seen before or since. We were also close to Rino Sanders, a journalist and poet who became one of our beloved friends in Hamburg. At his home we met Günther Grass, Walter Busse, and other writers and artists—all extremely intelligent and gifted, hoping for and trying to create a better future. We also became good friends of Signe Jahnn, the daughter of the writer Hans-Henny Jahnn, who had left Germany in 1933 and returned with his family to Hamburg after the war.

Of course, it was difficult for us to leave behind these and other friends, chief among them the kind and loving Wachmanns and the Schreibers, but we had no doubt that to create a new, meaningful world for ourselves, we had to go to the United States. We knew that the invitation of Pista was a great honor for him and that he could look forward to a life in America in which he would be well-known in his field, satisfied regarding his work, and highly appreciated.

28

New Life

We left Hamburg in November 1962. Our plane flew from Bremen to New York, and the next plane from New York to Austin. We were again unimaginably happy. I had not only healed from my earlier depression; I was full of expectation about arriving in a country where my father had always yearned to live. It was a country, I was told, where people were truly free and where we would not be hated or persecuted because we were Jewish or because my father had a pharmacy and a serum laboratory. We would not have to worry about whether we had a job because if we were seriously looking, we could find one. I hoped for so much in America, especially that my parents would come one day and see how happy and well we were here. I even believed that seeing our lives in the United States, they would decide to come and stay here forever.

Austin was both overwhelming and quiet. It was neither crowded nor did it offer as much amusement as it does today. It was a hub of intense intellectual activity with an intimate, small-town flavor. The department of physics as well as the department of mathematics had just started to grow significantly, employing some of the most famous American and European mathematicians and physicists of the time. The chairman of the newly developing research group in general relativity was Alfred Schild, who had attracted to his department a number of young scholars such as Roy Kerr, Roger Penrose, Jürgen Ehlers, István, Engelbert, and others. Pista, too, could hardly wait to start his research and teaching. Soon after our arrival I went to the German department to talk to the current head, Helmuth Rehder, who approved of my plan to enroll in the school's PhD program, which I did. Having loved reading and studying German literature since childhood, I was delighted by my new field of study. I had classes on Goethe, Schiller, and Thomas Mann and studied the histories of Old High German, early medieval German, and the country itself from its beginnings to the present day, including its achievements over the centuries in literature, music, and the arts. I enjoyed every minute of my classes and readings.

My depression was gone. I looked excitedly forward to our new life, knowing that it would be wonderful. While the pressure of having abandoned my parents and the fear that I might not see them again did not leave me, I learned to live with this knowledge and even to be happy despite my concerns. In fact, everything that happened to us gave me tremendous hope. I believed that later we would be able to see them more often and that the pressure of communism would change and even decrease after a while.

Figure 11. My mother, Gitta Abonyi (née Nagy).

I no longer worried about Pista's future either: he was happy with the research he had undertaken with Engelbert, and he was highly appreciated at the university. He also published a number of articles and enjoyed teaching. Being employed by an excellent American university, he could look forward to a highly promising future, and we were both happy about his studies in his new field, which fascinated him and which he loved. Nor did I worry about my own future. I knew that I would be as deeply interested and involved in studying German culture and German literature as I had been with my musical career. At the same time I did not feel that I had abandoned music, because I had not. It was just that my life ceased to revolve around my piano playing.

As for our marriage, we lived as before my fall into depression: in love with one another, relishing our life. We enjoyed the freedom we had never experienced before and saw that all doors were open to us in any place, in any direction we would want to go. We felt that there was no limit to our hopes for the future, seeing our horizon larger and larger, having insights heretofore unknown to us.

Of course, there was no change in the refusal of the Hungarian Communist state to issue passports to my father and mother, no hope for change in the near future. But my outlook on life changed, and I started to believe Pista, who had always said, "Things might become different in

Hungary from one minute to another." That is, I started to hope that one day a miracle would occur: Hungary would be free again and my parents would be able to come and stay with us forever.

In long discussions about our future, Pista said that he knew that he would get a permanent job either in Austin or at another American university. At that time there were plenty of jobs for scholars in the natural sciences, so we were not concerned about what would happen. Also, he was truly happy and deeply immersed in his work. While I still hoped that my parents would get passports, I no longer contemplated the idea of going back to Hungary. I learned to deal with the reality of the present. Cured of my misery, our marriage was happier than ever before; we both stood with feet firmly on the ground, looking forward to a happy life and a successful future.

* * *

Pista was eventually offered jobs at several universities, but he became really excited when Ivor Robinson called him to Dallas. Ivor, a friend of Engelbert, had visited us in Hamburg during the summer of 1962, and he and Pista became very much interested in the work of each other, passionately discussing it day and night. At the time, Ivor was a visiting professor at Syracuse University. While there, he received a job offer from Dallas, Texas, where a new research institute was opening its doors. This new institute had been supported by the regents of Texas Instruments, the large firm that decided to create a scientific center in Dallas, which they wanted to be comparable in reputation and influence to the Institute for Advanced Studies at Princeton. Since at this point initiatives like this one were picked up and supported by such government agencies as the National Science Foundation, the Graduate Research Center of the Southwest opened its doors in Richardson, Dallas at the beginning of the 1960s.

At this point it was our friend Ivor Robinson, who had been hired by Lloyd Berkner, one of the leading physicists of Texas Instruments, to create a department of relativists, theoretical physicists, and mathematicians to work in these and related fields. Ivor believed that he could build up a significant relativity group in this new institution. The ambition of the major movers of Texas Instruments, Eric Johnson (later the Mayor of Dallas) and his partners, was to create one of the country's best research institutions in the natural sciences. Lloyd Berkner, the American physicist and one of the leading contributors of the theory of short wave radio propagation, became the director of the institution. He also described with L. C. Marshall a theory of the way in which the atmospheres of the solar systems' inner planets had evolved. Ivor invited Pista from Austin, Michael Cohen from Bruxelles, and Wolfgang Rindler from Cornell University in Ithaca. Over the next few years, a number of well-known scholars were offered jobs and came to Dallas to work at the Graduate Research Center. Pista knew some of them from the Jordan Seminar in Hamburg, such as Klaus Bichteler, Manfred Trümper, and Jürgen Ehlers. Others we met upon their arrival in Dallas, among them two internationally known scholars, Roger Penrose from England and Yuval Nee'man from Israel. Within a few more years, other scholars came as well, and the Center became a well-known institution all over the world. In the early 1980s it was taken over by the State of Texas, which renamed it the University of Texas at Dallas. A few years later this institution added several new fields to its programs and became a full-fledged university.

* * *

We arrived in Dallas in the summer of 1963. Ivor was waiting for us at the airport, and without delay we went to his house for dinner. I remember it was a great dinner: fried beef, lamb chops, potatoes, salad, spinach, and apple cake. We enjoyed the food and were truly happy! By the time we arrived in Ivor's apartment, a number of Pista's new colleagues were there: they were waiting for our arrival. It was thus that our decades-long celebration with our friends began. The circle we at first belonged to consisted of some very nice and very intelligent people, most of whom were physicists and mathematicians; later, a number of musicians, artists, writers, historians, and literary scholars joined their ranks. It was a large group of close friends just like before in Hungary or in Germany. And when we had children they, their parents, and their friends also belonged in our closest circle. This first night at Ivor's, we heard from them details about Dallas, about the most interesting events in town, the best housing, and the best schools in the area.

From that day on, we were invited practically every weekend to go out for lunch or to somebody's house for supper, or we played host to our friends. We learned about the lives of Pista's colleagues, about their previous jobs, and about American college life in addition to having animated political discussions with one another as well as discussions about music, literature, culture, and later about children. In this way, over the years we developed close relationships with these people, comparable on an "adult" level to the relationships we had had with my "Winnie the Pooh" playmates in Budapest and later with our friends in Hamburg. Indeed, our relationships with friends in Dallas were built, just like our previous friendships, on deep emotional affinity and intellectual exchange, foundations which have lasted a lifetime. I felt that we belonged here and that our friends were the best and kindest people on earth. Of course, I still yearned for my parents. But I understood that we could not go back to Hungary: such an act would not help them or us. Rather, I hoped for a time when some change in the Soviet bloc would allow people, at least people of their age, to leave Hungary. I knew I would have to learn to live without them at least for a while. Though I was sad about this, I was no longer crippled by despair.

*　*　*

While we spent the weekends with our friends, during the week I studied intensely for my degree. Travelling to Austin every week by train and returning by bus, I had to take four semesters' worth of courses in the German department. I had thought that I had a deep insight into German literature, but now I saw how little I knew. I did not know its connections with other literatures, and I did not see it in relation to its own past. I read and read and read and read. Exploring the German poetry of the Middle Ages as well as the fiction and poetry of the eighteenth, nineteenth, and twentieth centuries became some of the greatest artistic experiences of my life.

29

A Terrible Event

As usual, on Wednesday, November 20, 1963, I went to Austin, planning to return to Dallas that Friday. Since I had an early morning class on Fridays, I usually left Austin by plane, landing in Dallas around 1:00 P.M. But on the night of the twenty-first, Pista called me and said, "Come, Darling, earlier! We are invited together with the Robinsons, the Rindlers, and a number of others from our Institute for a luncheon with President Kennedy, who is coming to Dallas for a day! And we have to be at the Trade Mart by 11:15 or 11:30 A.M. at the latest."

"Really?" I was delighted! "What a wonderful plan!"

I rearranged my ticket for an earlier flight on Friday morning: I didn't go to my class but took a taxi to the airport and flew to Dallas. I arrived. Pista was waiting for me at the airport, and we went home. Leaving our apartment around 10:30 A.M., we drove to the Trade Mart and arrived there around 11:15. As we went inside, I noticed that we were quite close to the podium. At our table we met the Robinsons, the Rindlers, and other friends and colleagues of Pista from the Graduate Research Center. Looking around, I saw a huge and colorful crowd sitting there, eagerly waiting for the big moment: the arrival of the President of the United States. Involved as always in big discussions with friends around the table, we, too, were excitedly waiting for the Kennedys. Time went by, but they didn't arrive. In fact, 12:00 noon passed. We were talking about the various school systems in the States when suddenly, the waiters started to bring the salad. "What is happening?" I asked. "Why don't we wait for the President?"

"Well, don't worry," said Wolfgang Rindler, "he might be a bit late."

After a while, the waiter came back to pick up the plates. "What happened?" I asked him. "Why are we eating?"

He looked at me, then pointing to his head, he said, "Bang, bang!" And he left.

"What is this?" I turned to Ivor, "What horrible behavior is this?"

"Don't worry! Sometimes people are strange," was his answer.

After a while the waiter returned. "What happened?" I asked him again, this time urgently.

Again he looked at me, and pointing to his head, he said again, "Bang, bang!"

"My goodness," I turned to the people at my table, "I can't stand this. What kind of answer is this?"

"Eat," was the answer. "He sees that it annoys you." By then it was almost 1:00 P.M., and people in the kitchen had listened to the radio and heard about the events that had taken place.

We ate our steaks. The hall was cold. At 1:00 P.M. (Kennedy had been shot at 12:30) J. Erik Jonsson went to the microphone: "A mishap has taken place," he said. "Keep your seats! As soon as we know what happened, we'll let you know."

The tension grew. Some people ate; most did not. A few minutes later, Erik Jonsson came again to the podium: "President Kennedy and Governor Connally have been shot," he said. The twenty-five hundred people in the Trade Mart stared at him, dumbfounded.

At this point the Reverend Luther Holcomb came to the microphone and led the room in prayer.

Some people took the flowers from the vases on their tables. Moving slowly, we left the Trade Mart. The plaza around us was black from the large number of police filling up the space, as if a huge black carpet and black curtains covered everything.

We went home. For the next three days we were sitting in front of the radio: we were paralyzed. I told Pista again and again, "The world hasn't changed: as we did in Hungary, we are still sitting in front of the radio listening to devastating news."

We still couldn't believe it.

30

Becoming Parents

While the shock of President Kennedy's assassination has never left me to this day, slowly our lives recuperated. In fact, in January 1964, when I discovered that I was pregnant, I suddenly felt as though my entire life had been heading toward this previously unimaginable fulfillment. Having the most beautiful, tender feelings, a previously unknown pleasure and happiness, I was overwhelmed by my love for Pista, for my parents, and for this gorgeous new baby, whom I would meet shortly. Grateful to Pista for having gone through those horrible months of depression with me and being again deeply in love with him, I saw the world as repaired, rich and good to both of us. And I had every reason for seeing it this way. By then we had loved one another for fourteen years. Nothing had changed; at this point in our life, as before, we could not wait to arrive home and embrace one another, talking about everything that happened to us during the day. Feeling tremendous delight and happiness in his presence I felt constant pleasure in living with him, enjoying his humor, his intoxicating love for me, his goodness, and his grateful humanity. Indeed, he was happy and open, taking me in his arms again and again.

He kept up a close relationship with his parents as well. He missed them, and like me he had pangs of conscience for having left them. Writing one or two letters to Kölesd every week, he told them again and again how happy we would be if they could come to Dallas and stay with us. They were, however, afraid of the long journey and told us in no uncertain terms that they would not want to come to the United States but rather would love to meet us in Europe. Nor did Pista forget about his relationship with my father, whom he adored, and my mother, whom he regarded as his second mother. He missed them and tried to do everything possible to help them obtain the passports for which they applied over and over again without result. But then suddenly, just a short while after I found out that I was pregnant, I heard the news from my parents: unbelievably, both had received passports to America.

How did this happen? A couple of months before, my father had been told by a high-ranking official who knew about the inner workings of the Hungarian government agencies that in the Hungarian People's Republic one was more likely to secure a passport after retirement than while employed in a position of importance and responsibility. Within a month of hearing this, my father retired. He was sixty-six years old, an age when most Hungarians were already retired. The government official's words were accurate. Soon after my father retired both of my parents received their passports. Miracle of miracles. They planned to come to Dallas in August 1964, three weeks after our baby Kathleen was to be born. At this point we agreed that life was beautiful and incredibly good to us.

Indeed Pista and I were deeply in love, celebrating every minute of the day. Our happy marriage, the birth of our child, and our unimaginably rich and beautiful world, in addition to the miracle of my parents' visit, reminded us constantly how good life was to us. Also, Pista was professionally happy to work within the field of relativity with great colleagues, living in peace and loving me more than ever. For the first time in our lives we were unafraid of the future, and he was no longer being forced to work on something he did not like. We looked forward to every minute of our day with great expectation. At the same time, despite my pregnancy, during the latter part of fall 1963 and spring 1964 I travelled weekly to Austin and was able to finish my coursework during the first summer semester.

Little Kathleen arrived on August 3. Her birth, her sweetness, Pista's love for her, and my own previously unimaginable happiness marked my life forever. Pista sometimes spent hours sitting next to her bed or her pram, looking at her in loving amazement such as I had never seen before. He smiled when he saw her and told me again and again how happy he was with her in the world and how much he loved her. Each time he saw her, he would whisper that she was a miracle, a star from heaven, an angel, and the greatest pleasure on earth. Indeed, Kathleen was delightful and beautiful: she had large gray-blue eyes, light skin, and blond hair, resembling my mother and relatives of her family. Sometimes she also looked like Iván and like Iván's little daughter Kriszti. In addition, she was incredibly sweet and loving, and we could not fathom that she was ours. Pista's eyes were often full of tears, and sometimes he would laugh for a long time enjoying the sight of her, her ways of watching the world, her activities, and her development.

And my parents were soon to arrive.

31

Pleasure and Grief

That they did not want to stay in Dallas forever was clear from the beginning. Emphasizing that they had come for a six-month-long visit, they insisted on planning their return to Hungary for January or February 1965. They did not want to leave their home to the state (had they stayed in America, their apartment and everything they owned would have been seized by the Hungarian authorities), nor did they want to leave Iván, their son, whom they would never see again. He was a young man of thirty-five and a doctor who would, they felt, never receive a passport to leave Hungary. They also surmised that if they were allowed to come once now that my father had retired, they would probably be able to come again. Both of them were sure that at this point, the Communist system was weaker than it had been even a few years ago. The very fact that they had received a passport was enough for them to believe

Figure 12. Zsuzsi, Peter, Kathleen, and Pista (2009).

that the system was slowly but surely deteriorating, a process that would bring at least in some respects a certain improvement of freedom in Hungary.

I had to admit to myself that their arguments made sense. My father, sixty-six years old, had already suffered one heart attack; he was neither young nor healthy enough to start a new business in America; and obviously, neither he nor my mother wanted to stay in a foreign country just to take care of the household and Kathleen while waiting for us to return from work. They imagined that after their visit, we would be able to meet every year. Hungary would depend less and less on the Soviet Union, and the whole system would collapse after a while(in the long run they were right, but their prediction regarding the change of the system didn't take place for another twenty-five years).

Still, we argued about this all the time—at home, in the street, at friends' houses, in Pista's office—everywhere. Despite these arguments, we had a wonderful time. Whatever I had ever believed in or had been hoping for had now become reality: we were no longer separated. I had even found a violinist, a violist, and a cello player whom I invited to our house to play chamber music with my father.

* * *

And then one day, exactly three weeks after my parents arrived, my father could not get up in the morning. Seeing that he was truly sick, I called Dr. Brian Williams, a heart specialist at Baylor Hospital whom I had consulted before my parents' arrival to make sure that he would see my father during their time in Dallas. I called him and he came to our apartment immediately. He said that my father needed to be taken to Baylor Hospital because he feared that it was a heart attack. Pista took him in an ambulance to Baylor while I drove my mother and baby Kathleen to the hospital. Within four hours, my father had died of a massive heart attack.

We were crushed. I had been afraid of this catastrophe throughout my childhood, throughout the Holocaust—indeed, my whole life. I had feared that he would be killed like almost everybody else in our family, like the fathers of almost all the children I had known in Békéscsaba and Budapest. In my nightmares I saw him murdered again and again. And I had never become free of this vision. It was and has always been part of my life.

But my father died in Dallas, Texas, and he had had such a difficult, pain-laden life. He had been drafted in World War I as an eighteen-year-old. Shot in the head, he was lucky to survive without brain injury. He lost his beloved brother and sister in the Holocaust. Yet he survived together with us during the intense, four-month-long Siege of Budapest in the fall and winter of 1944 and 1945, including the starvation periods that followed. Yet despite his humiliation and suffering, he was so good and loving. In fact, besides István I have never seen anyone like him in my life. He adored his family, cared about all of his friends, and helped everybody who needed it. And my mother? She lost the last witness to her life, her support, her love, her hope, her ideal. And we, Iván, Pista, and I lost our father, whose entire life consisted of his love for and dedication to us. I have never gotten over his loss, nor did Pista, who when mentioning him always had tears in his eyes.

* * *

My mother, too, mourned his death for as long as she lived. She stayed in Dallas until the end of June of 1965. During this time I learned to cook by just watching her and reading her cookbooks. I finally understood her statement and underlying advice: "If one knows how to read, one knows how to cook." I needed this. Together with me, Pista also learned the "secrets."

From that time on I cooked whenever we invited people, preparing my favorite Hungarian dishes, most of which I had not eaten since I left Hungary. At this point, however, they became part of our most frequent dinner menus for many years to come. And while I cooked dinner, Pista washed the dishes and cleaned the kitchen. In fact one of his well-known "complaints" to our guests was that "everybody praises the supper, but nobody talks about how clean the plates are!"

After supper, with our guests around, when we went into the living room to sit down and discuss the events of the day, he often lay down under the piano and drew mathematical formulae, getting involved in our discussion only at some later point. Sometimes he even fell asleep. When awakening, he would immediately become involved in our discussions and remark quietly, "Sorry, but only in good company can one fall asleep."

Often he was discussing and arguing all night. He loved these evenings with our friends. He also learned from my mother how to make bread. My mother had inherited this recipe from her mother, and we celebrated each time she baked it. No doubt this bread is a matchless creation: sprinkled with caraway seeds, soft on the inside, crunchy on the outside with a heavenly taste that is almost impossible to describe. While our children were at home, Pista baked it three times a week; after they left, just once a week. In fact, to the delight of our family and our friends, from the summer of 1964

Figure 13. Physicists Ivor Robinson, Roger Penrose, Engelbert Schücking, Jürgen Ehlers, István Ozsváth, Peter Ozsváth, and Tibor Herczeg at a conference in Dallas (date unknown).

throughout our life in Dallas, this bread was the most beloved food in our lives. It brought the greatest delight to us every day as well as to our guests, many of whom have its recipe and bake it regularly.

* * *

In the summer of 1965, all of us flew to Vienna to meet with Pista's parents, Erzsi, my brother Iván, his wife Mari, and their sweet little eight-year-old daughter Krisztina. None of them had received a passport to visit the West before, which meant that we had not seen any of them during the seven years since we left Hungary. Living for decades within closed borders, our entire family was now able to get passports. At this point we believed that all of them would follow us to the United States, where we had secured entrance papers for everybody, including Pista's parents. Since the whole family would have had to ask the United States for asylum and wait as long as it took to validate their papers, each of them was invited by Ivor's parents to Liverpool, England. The Robinsons had heard about the waiting period and offered their house for our relatives to stay in as long as needed. We knew that it might take as long as a year. In addition, we arranged that after they arrived in Dallas, Iván would have a job as a research scientist at Southwestern Medical School, which would provide a satisfying lifestyle and fulfilling work until he finished his medical licensing exams. That is, he could earn money as a research scientist and support his family until he passed the exams.

But despite the opportunities offered to them, no one came back with us from Europe.

I understood Pista's parents: they were in their sixties, spoke no other language but Hungarian, and had done nothing else in their lives but farm work. They would have a hard time finding anything of that sort even in Budapest, let alone in Dallas. Erzsi and my mother also spoke no English, and they couldn't imagine living here and depending on the two of us for the rest of their lives. Iván, of course, was a different case: had he come, he could have learned English within two or three years, passed his exams, and made an excellent living. But he wasn't ready to do this, nor was his wife Mari, who felt bound to Hungary. Overcome by emotions, she felt intensely that she could not leave behind her parents and her homeland.

After this meeting with our families, we left Vienna—alone. No one came with us. I was sad about their reaction and sickened by their arguments. So was Pista.

"They don't know what it means to live in freedom and dignity," he said. He was right: they did not. But what could we do about it? They felt that they had made the right decision, and who were we to tell them that they had not?

After this meeting with everybody in the summer of 1965, we went for a visit to our friends in Germany and came back to Dallas deeply disappointed.

32

At Home

In 1969, we bought a house. When we arrived in Dallas in 1963, several of our friends advised us to buy a house as quickly as possible.

"I don't want a house," I told Pista after we discussed the issue with several of our friends. "I don't want anything that could be taken away from us!"

"For heaven's sake, who would take it away?" he asked. "Almost everybody has a house."

"One never knows the answer to such questions," I remarked. "I've had enough of owning something and then having to run away and part from it."

"Well," he said, "we'll have to live in America for a while to get you used to the fact that you won't have to run away from here!"

We finally bought one in 1969, built on a completely new street. It took years for us to finish furnishing it because we wanted to have very simple teakwood furniture, books, and a piano to "replace our treasures" we had left in Budapest. Throughout all those years, I never thought that in addition to my beautiful marriage and wonderful children, I could ever have a home again, but I suddenly had one. Feeling that I had arrived in heaven, I gained a house in a world in which I was happy and felt once more at home.

At this point Pista started to create a garden. Planting new trees, grass, bushes, and flowers, he made everything with his own hands. In fact he created a beautiful garden of rich colors and buoyant growth; it was a lifelong project. Working hard in it until the last days of his life, he achieved the most astonishing success.

We now had a happy life, a beautiful home, and a beautiful garden. But the wounds of the past did not heal completely: my father had died, and our loved ones still lived in Hungary.

* * *

In 1970 we all met again in Vienna. This time we did not have a job offer for Iván. And, of course, he did not need one. In fact he claimed to be happy in Hungary and explained how the system had changed, how everything was easier in the country than it had been in the past—even how simple it was today for people to get passports. Also, he claimed again and again that he had a well-paid, highly appreciated position and that the restrictions of the past had more or less disappeared from everyday life. This was true on the point of unmitigated terror but not on the point of freedom, dreams for the future, inventing one's own life, living without fear, and raising children. But what could we have done? The same arguments were repeated, but nobody was willing to move to America. Two weeks later we flew to Denmark, where Pista had a conference on relativity. When it was over we returned to the United States. This was the last time I saw my mother. Six months later, she also died of a heart attack.

My poor mother! She had a horrendous life. During the early thirties because of raging inflation, she had had to leave Szabadka, the town where she grew up, and move with my father, Iván, and me to Békéscsaba, a new town where she knew nobody and it was hard for her to make new friends. I understand it now: she was very lonely. Also, she had to face the growing antisemitism in the country and live through my father's loss of his business, which by 1941 had become the object of the Hungarian anti-Jewish laws. At this point she had to move again. Since she knew only a few people in Budapest as well, she lived a pretty lonely existence there, too. Then came 1944, and she lived through the atrocities of the German invasion. She also learned about the deportation and eventual murder of her brother and all her sisters. In addition, she survived months of devastating hunger during the Siege of Budapest, years of poverty, the terror of the new Communist rule, my leaving the country, and finally my father's death. She died of heart failure when she was seventy-one years old. By then she was completely broken, and I had not been able to do anything to make her life easier.

* * *

Going back to the end of 1965, I should mention that I finished my coursework in Austin. What followed was my dissertation. Writing a study on Goethe, Schiller, and Thomas Mann, I received my PhD in 1968. At that time it was not as difficult to land a job at a university as it is today, but with me there was a problem: I had no flexibility. Yes, there were several job openings all over the country, but I felt that I was nailed to Dallas. First,

Pista was here. He felt productive, was working well, and was happy in his job. Also, he was in the company of an outstanding group of scientists at the Graduate Research Center of the Southwest (today the University of Texas at Dallas), all working with great enthusiasm and intensity. In addition, we had a large number of friends in Dallas with whom we shared a life comparable to our life in Budapest. Of course, I was not playing games anymore, but we had close friends to share the events of our life and the great promise of the future. At this point we had constant and great discussions on child-rearing, babies, teenagers in Europe and in America, psychology, schools, world politics, the Russians' plans for Europe, America's reaction to them, the wars, the Holocaust, new music, new literature, and other important contemporary events. We lived in nice homes without the threat of losing them to the state or having everything taken from us at any moment. Finding security and being more at home here than anywhere before in our lives, we were truly happy in Dallas. I did not want to try out other places. The research institute was excellent in Pista's field: he read and wrote all day, intensely discussing mathematics with colleagues who highly respected him. It was obvious to me that insisting on going to a place unknown to us both would be a bad idea. In fact, forcing Pista into yet another surrounding only because I wanted to find a job for myself made no sense. It is important to emphasize that it was I in the first place who did not have the strength to leave Dallas, my first real home since Budapest, a place with great friends and relationships. Nor did I have the courage to drag Pista away from the job he enjoyed tremendously and the place where he was truly happy. We decided that we would stay in Dallas and that I should try to get a job in the city. Even if I did not get one right away, I probably would do so in the future. Of course, this was not an easy task—especially in the field of German literature and culture.

* * *

This concern came up, however, only after my graduation from the University of Texas at Austin in 1968. On October 20, 1967, a new miracle came into our lives: two-and-a-half months after Kathleen's third birthday, we had another baby, and there was no limit to our happiness. With his large brown eyes, dark hair, delightfully sweet smile, and happy temperament, Peter reminded me of Pista, my father, and his relatives. He also radiated, like Kathleen, a special sweetness and intelligence, the likes of which I have rarely seen in my life. By then Kathleen played all kinds of fascinating games: she invented wonderful stories, put together puzzles of over one hundred pieces, listened to and was enchanted by the fairy tales I would tell her all the time; but she also liked hearing me tell sweet little stories to Peter, inventing some on her own as well. Indeed, she had a remarkably loving relationship with Peter: delighted by her little brother and proud of his admiration of her, they played happily together. In addition, both children were deeply dedicated to music. At the age of seven Kathleen started taking violin lessons and within a year played beautifully, musically, and with amazing virtuosity. Yet I was a bit afraid of her performance. While I would always praise her, I never told her that she had an extraordinary talent for the violin, afraid as I was of passing on to her my own, somewhat negative experience of planning and then giving up a career in music.

But she won first place in a violin competition with a friend of hers, April Wheeler, and their prize was to play with the Dallas Youth Orchestra. The two young girls played the Bach Double Violin Concerto in a concert as well. Pista was enormously happy and proud of her, telling me he felt that his life had been completely fulfilled. Although he did not grow up listening to music, he had an exceptional sense of its beauty and form, listening to me practice the great pieces of piano literature for decades and then proudly listening to his children's performances, enjoying their extraordinary talent in music.

Kathleen also loved to sew. Learning this art from a friend of mine, she sewed many beautiful skirts, blouses, jackets, and dresses for herself from the age of ten. In fact, when she got married she sewed the dresses of her bridesmaids. All of us were amazed. Then, one day she watched one of the first televised heart operations with us. She might have been ten or twelve years old. Sitting breathlessly in our living room, she called out at the end, "This is what I want to do when I grow up! I want to be a surgeon." From that time on she watched every television show involving heart operations and said each time she saw one, "this is what I want to become when I grow up: a surgeon." And this is what she has become: today Kathleen is a vascular surgeon at Albany Medical Hospital.

Back then she lived happily within our family; she was much loved and admired. But then from the fourth grade on, she started to be disgruntled in school. Yearning for acceptance and popularity among her peers, she felt essentially different from the rest. Indeed we had never been to a football match, had never even seen one, nor did we know about its importance in other people's lives. We also didn't know what girls did on such occasions.

We listened to Beethoven, Bach, and Mozart at home rather than to popular music. In addition, we would read the European classics rather than go dancing to the music of the 1970s and 1980s. We knew nothing of this culture.

"Why is it so wrong to be different?" I kept on asking, completely amazed.

Indeed there was a cultural difference between us and the others, which we did not immediately understand. I had been different in Hungary, too, but I had been proud of it and so were my parents, precisely *because* I was different. Of course, when I was young I had two or three close friends who read the same books, listened to the same music, played the same games, and were like me: very much aware of the fact that we were different. So while I was used to this notion, I missed seeing that being different in America was not the same as being different in Hungary. István missed this point, too. To him as to me, "otherness" meant having a great advantage rather than a sense of shame. But this I only understood after many years of watching Kathleen's experience in school. It was a very difficult time for all three of us. Kathleen cried rather often, and I went in vain to the teachers and school principals, attempting to figure out what was wrong. Pista, too, tried his best to ease the situation, but neither of us was successful. Only much later did we understand that Kathleen was being teased and bullied in school because she was in many ways unlike the rest, and in this situation, nobody took her side. We, her parents, were later filled with sorrow for not realizing this sooner. Yet apparently in the long run, not much damage was done: Kathleen is one of the most loving daughters I have ever seen or known in my life.

* * *

On the other hand, Peter showed no interest in being like the rest. He was happy with his few friends—the children of our friends—and they would invent all kinds of games to play. He had his playmates and was quite happy in the world.

Interestingly enough, unlike Kathleen and me he showed no interest in fairy tales. In fact he would always check my stories, asking me emphatically before he lay down for the night not to tell him anything that was "not true," only stories and events that "were true." As early as age two his interests reminded me very much of Pista's approach to the world. Rather than playing with the various toys we bought him from the wonderful toy stores in town, he liked to watch insects, compulsively looking for them all over the garden. He would watch their movements hour after hour, both inside the house and outside, sometimes all day. He studied for years the world of bugs, an interest which he later extended to all kinds of animals but especially to turtles, birds, dinosaurs, fish, and snakes.

"Tell me only true stories," he would say when I tucked him into bed at night.

Likewise, when he got a bit older he wanted to talk, read, and learn more about a variety of animals he discovered in the books we found in the bookstores of Dallas. For many years to come he would study their lives, always choosing just one kind of insect or one kind of animal for long discussions. Only after several days or weeks, sometimes even months of reading and discussions could we talk or read about a new insect or a new bird rather the one we had by then been discussing for a long, long time. When I mentioned this to Pista he was happy and proud, because as a child he, too, had always been interested in only one thing at a time, speaking about it, reading about it, and dreaming about it at night. He also told me that it would annoy him to no end when people stopped talking about what he wanted to discuss. It was perhaps not amazing that Peter and Pista were so similar to one another.

Peter would also draw pictures of the creatures we were reading about; he drew them on paper in hundreds of forms, endlessly discussing and drawing their habits and inclinations. He drew pictures of other things as well, wonderful caricatures of people and animals alike. He listened to music while we played, conducting recordings of Mozart piano concertos and Beethoven symphonies. First he studied piano, and at eleven he began to play the cello. In fact he has remained a passionate cellist to this day, organizing chamber music nights and performing at home as often as possible.

In elementary and middle school, he was not very popular. Many children thought him strange, not knowing how to deal with his preoccupation with insects, his interest in classical music, his lack of interest in sports, and other popular activities. One day when I picked him up from third grade, he whispered to me to keep quiet and leave as fast as we could.

"Why," I asked softly in Hungarian.

"Because I have a matchbox in my pocket," he whispered, "with a scorpion in it!"

It was only in high school that he found some close friends and peers. Of course, he always had two or three childhood playmates who enjoyed his company among the children of Pista's colleagues as well. But in tenth grade the physics teacher recommended that Peter and several of his classmates begin to meet in each other's homes twice a week to think about, research, and discuss issues in physics they found interesting. He became close to all of these kids. He also took various math and computer science classes at the University of Texas at Dallas (UTD) with Pista, who accompanied him everywhere. When he was fifteen years old he started to work in one of the computer labs belonging to the owner of a new computer firm who knew him from UTD and who had just started his own business. There Peter was highly valued. He worked twice a week for three or four hours, earning significant sums of money.

Peter also played the cello and practiced seriously in addition to studying composition with Robert Rodriguez, a composer friend of ours at UTD. He played chamber music and was involved with the Dallas Youth Orchestra. In addition, he played math games with Pista. In fact, all the time they talked about math and computer science and had a wonderful time together.

Pista also spent much time with Kathleen: they would joke, play, and assemble endless jigsaw puzzles together, often working on puzzles of seven hundred pieces or more. He also enjoyed Kathleen's questions about the development of the earth, her violin-playing, and her talent in music. Life was a great pleasure for us with both children. From the first grade to the twelfth, Pista took them to and from school every day, and when I protested and claimed that I could help by doing my share (to say nothing of the school buses actively functioning in our neighborhood), he would protest:

"Let me do this. I enjoy being with them so much." I let him, of course, and so he did—as many as four times a day for fifteen years.

I, on the other hand, would practice with Kathleen for her violin lessons. Her intonation was impeccable, and she played with a rarely heard, natural musicality. I also read to her Hungarian fairy tales and, when she grew older, some of the most beautiful novels written for young people from Hungarian, English, or French literature. All this time I felt that Peter and Kathleen were bringing back to me not only my childhood but also the "fairy tale play time" I had enjoyed with my friends in Budapest.

Delighted by the beauty and riches of our life, Pista often told me that he never knew what playing and happiness meant until then. He was delighted to live in this world of games and fairy tales he could only imagine as a child.

We spoke Hungarian at home so that both of the children learned two languages: one at home and the other in school and with friends, becoming fluent in both. However, all the books we read to them were in Hungarian. We also taught them a number of the great Hungarian poems, many of which they learned by heart. Little Kathleen knew large parts of János Arany's *Toldy* in addition to a number of Petőfi, Ady, and Radnóti poems. Pista was a wonderful role model in this respect as well. As a child he had learned by heart for his own pleasure some of the most beautiful Hungarian poems, many of which he taught Kathleen to recite. One day when she must have been ten or eleven years old, we decided to teach her some English poems as well, since she never learned any of the great English poets' work in school. We introduced her to Shakespeare, Keats, and Shelley, and after an hour of explaining and reciting the poems we had chosen we promised her that for next time, we'd find some new poems to recite. This plan pleased her.

"Wonderful! Do so!" she said. "This was truly a fabulous time: I didn't know that people wrote beautiful poems in English as well."

Pista also taught both children to build complicated constructions with LEGO, to play with trains, and most importantly he passed on the concept of putting together small pieces to create something larger and completely unexpected. He deeply appreciated every single toy, perhaps because he never had a toy as a child—such objects were lacking in the homes of Hungarian farmers during the 1930s—or simply because he loved to play. He was awed by what he saw in the stores. He would constantly buy new toys and bring them back to Kathleen and Peter. Then he would sit on the floor every evening and play with them for hours, putting together new rooms, dollhouses, bridges, gardens, and all sorts of machines.

Kathleen loved to swim, so Pista went swimming with her every morning before school, and they did this for many years.

At the same time, Peter was fascinated by extinct animals. For years and years, dinosaurs were at the center of his thinking. Pista encouraged him to read and learn more about them, always finding new books and new information about the world of these ancient creatures. As I mentioned, he was delighted by Peter's concentration on only one animal or only one event at a time. He believed this was the best way to understand something deeply and get as close to the issue as possible. He would say it repeatedly: "Peter truly has a one-track mind!"

Pista had the same quirk. Except when talking to me from his heart about his deepest emotions or reciting poetry, he would also concentrate on one issue at a time and not want to think or talk about anything else.

But it was not only science that moved Pista to the core. He was happy to spend hours with Kathleen as well. He adored her. Aware of the difference in the nature and interests of the two children, he always did what they wanted him to do. He believed that he should encourage them to follow their own interests, for to push them in the direction of their parents' interests was not right.

"Children must do whatever they would like to do," he would say. To him everything about them was a miracle as well as a great responsibility, so he surrounded them with toys and whatever interested them. He believed that our task was to make everything they wanted to become a part of our lives.

He also was aware of our turning the real world into one of playful freedom, and he thought, like me, that we would be able to live in both worlds, playing and loving to the end of our lives.

33

Teaching and Fulfillment

Wanting a job in town, I found one at Bishop College in downtown Dallas. I taught German for three hours a day, four days a week and was happy with my job, which was just perfect for me. I had every afternoon free for Kathleen, who was in kindergarten from nine to noon, and Peter, who went to day care for the same three hours a day. I was at home by 12:30.

* * *

But as time passed, the paradise in which we lived began to pale a bit. Kathleen was having a difficult time socially in middle school. She obviously wanted to be like the other children but was not, since we had a different lifestyle from most families in her school. This difference, which was appreciated at the university and by our friends, caused problems in the life of a child going to middle and high school in Dallas during the late 1970s and early 1980s. She was quite unhappy, and we were worried about her. We did not feel that we needed to change, nor did we know how. We saw that she was unhappy, but we did not know what to do about it. She was in tenth grade when she chose a boyfriend who was interested in football, baseball, and popular music. She changed into a young girl we had not seen before, acting as her boyfriend and her classmates did. Tensions grew at home, although we never quite understood what happened. Afraid of alienating rather than helping her, we were passive and said nothing about our feelings, which were nonetheless obviously written on our faces. I did everything to keep Pista quiet, fearing the tension that would explode when talking about the problem. We lived with this tension for two or three years. After her high school graduation Kathleen enrolled at Emory University, where her boyfriend followed her. Pista was quite desperate, but I knew that we were incapable of changing anything.

After a year their affair ended, however, and Kathleen graduated from Emory two years later. At this point she returned to Dallas, taking courses at UTD and starting to work at the university's biology program. But just before she was to receive her master's degree, she was accepted as a student at Southwestern Medical School. At this time she lived in Dallas, and we saw her only during the weekends. After graduation she married Gary Bernardini, another young doctor, and the couple moved to New York to complete their education. As I have mentioned, Kathleen has become a vascular surgeon and is now a professor at Albany Medical School. She has remained our beloved daughter, our pride, and our pleasure. We are also proud of Gary, who is a neurologist, heading the Department of Neurology at Weill Cornell Medical College in New York. They have a daughter just turning fifteen—a clever, sweet, and beautiful girl who is happy with her life and never shocks or resists her parents. She is named Elizabeth, after our sister Erzsébet (Erzsi) from Hungary.

* * *

Peter had it easier in high school. There were a few kids like him, and they became his friends. He also had friends from the youth orchestra in which Kathleen had played. Faced with the choice between the cello and mathematics for his professional life, he chose the latter. After his BS from Stanford University, he enrolled at Princeton as a graduate student. Today he is a full professor of mathematics at Princeton University and plays as much chamber music with his wife Shevi (also a musician) as their time allows. The couple lives in Princeton with their four sweet daughters: Eliana, Tamar, Nina, and Leora.

* * *

At Bishop College, where I taught German, I saw for the first time in my life how adults learn a foreign language, a process I knew nothing about since I had learned both languages I knew, German and English, as a child. I also met some interesting and intelligent students and colleagues at Bishop, among them Marta Satz, who became my friend for a lifetime. However, in 1978, ten years after my start there, the place landed in financial trouble, and I made a serious effort to find a job elsewhere. Of course, it was at Pista's workplace, the University of Texas at Dallas, where I hoped to be lucky enough to find one. This institution, originally called the Graduate Research Center of the Southwest when we came to Dallas and where Pista started to work in 1963, became part of the University of Texas system in 1967.

At first the new university offered only graduate classes to students in the sciences. It was not until 1975 that its humanities program started, and even then the place accepted only juniors and seniors. It would be some years before the place became a full-fledged university and the nepotism rule was relaxed—initially, two spouses could not work at the same university. Later the rule allowed the partners of faculty members to teach only if they taught in different departments, but by the early 1980s even this rule was erased for good. In 1979, a year after I stopped teaching at Bishop, I became a lecturer in the School of Arts and Humanities, teaching two German classes at UTD. It took some additional years before I started to publish and would begin to teach a variety of courses in the fields of literature and the history of ideas, concentrating on the Holocaust. I became an assistant professor in the 1980s and later was promoted to tenured associate professor, then finally to full professor. For the past twenty-five years, I have also been one of three professors in UTD's Holocaust Studies Program, a field and a program now recognized not only in Dallas but all over the country and other parts of the world.

Whenever I talk about my professional life, I must also mention Pista. Throughout our marriage he always encouraged me. He took pride in my piano playing at the beginning of our relationship and when I played in concerts. He was proud of me when I received my PhD and when I became professor at UTD. Also, he carefully read each of my publications and enjoyed discussing my ideas with me. He took great pleasure in reading my colleague Fred Turner's poetry and our translations of Goethe and the great Hungarian poets: Radnóti, Attila József, and others. It was a pure delight to talk with him about the literary, aesthetic, historical or political questions which have intensely occupied me my whole life, especially those regarding poetry and the Holocaust. His logical mind and tremendous insight helped me gain a deeper understanding of all these issues.

* * *

As for his professional life, Pista was fulfilled and happy through all the years of his tenure at UTD, where he taught theoretical physics and mathematics.

As I understand it, he did his research on relativity theory and Riemannian geometry. Of course, I have no idea what these words mean, but I learned from a number of other theoretical physicists that Pista's findings were of great importance in this field. Yet however great his results, he was never complacent with his own research: he constantly studied, reread, and recalculated the analyses that he made with Engelbert and wrote more about them in new articles and in new books. He also hoped to discover ever newer and more important results. He did this not because he was vain and wanted more fame or success—in fact, he had plenty of both—but because he wanted to resolve all those questions in the field that still needed to be answered. In the final analysis, it was the search for these answers that excited him and kept him in a constant state of wonder and anticipation. It was the way he spent his life from the day I first met him to the day he died.

But what will happen now to his search for a "beautiful" solution? Who will solve the problems he regarded as urgent? Has science moved in other directions? And does the urge to find answers for them drive somebody else? Does this drive live in Peter as vividly as it did in Pista, despite the fact that Peter asks very different questions and is in a very different field of research? I think it does. The academic beginnings of father and son were dissimilar, though. All through his youth, Pista never really believed that he had the time and the freedom to become a "real" mathematician. Coming from Kölesd, searching for answers, and after a while giving up his desire to concentrate on mathematics at Eötvös Loránt University in Budapest and later at the Hamburg Observatory, he began to believe that he must give up his dream, thinking that he could not concentrate on the field in which he was most interested. But working with Engelbert, their successful collaboration, and our move to the United States seemed to straighten out these problems. Now he was well-known in his field: he had the freedom to work on whatever he wanted and study in the area of his choice. So he had lived his last two years in Hamburg and then several decades in Texas with great satisfaction, involved in exciting research, enjoying his freedom, loving his children, and being aware of his luck and our happiness.

34

Past and Present

There can be no doubt that in every aspect of our lives, we were enormously lucky. Besides our professional satisfaction, our marriage did not change: it remained as romantic and as beautiful as in the beginning. We loved one another as much and more than we had during our first summer in 1949. Dizzy in his presence, melting in his arms, I was delighted by what he said, by his warmth, his way of seeing the world in a funny-grotesque light, and his limitless love and commitment to me and our children. In addition, I was happy about the previously unimaginable professional fulfillment in our lives, never forgetting where we had come from. In this way, while always looking toward the future for all of us, I never forgot my concern for my brother Iván and the living memory of my parents and their suffering; at this point in my life, I just tried to live with these memories. At the same time, I was sure that I would never again be afraid of the ideology of the state: whatever we had to go through, we would never again have to live as we had under the German and the Russian occupations of Hungary.

* * *

Time passed with unimaginable speed. Kathleen and Peter grew up and went to college. Their childhood ended, and we knew that what followed was important and would determine the course of their lives. Pista traveled with Kathleen to Emory University and, three years later, with Peter to Stanford University. We knew that we had to be happy about our children's goals and dreams and that we could not keep them back professionally, rather letting them stretch as far as they wish. Pista and I continued to live in Dallas. But our life was difficult without them: the loss of their everyday presence, which we had loved so passionately, meant that we lost the vitality, the rhythm, and the constantly intense emotions of our daily life. At the same time we also knew that however much we missed them, we could not change the future. Of course, we called them often, and they came home during vacations, yet after a while we understood that we had to give up—or at least deal better with—our intensive and constant longing for them. There was nothing else we could do: we simply had to let them go.

Occasionally I was envious of those of our friends whose children stayed in town, but I also knew that if we wanted to do the best for ours, we had to allow them to fly as high as they wanted to find their best chances, their future, and their luck. At the same time we found consolation in the promise of their professional lives, which opened up partly due to their choice of universities, partly due to their choice of profession, and partly of course to their great talents. We knew that their future in the places they went or wished to arrive would make them—and, therefore, all of us—happy. Also, it was important for us to remember that wherever they went, we would not be apart for long: we were still able to see them several times a year, which would console us. Still, we missed them tremendously and often spoke to each other about their painful absence in our everyday lives.

Perhaps it was harder on Pista than on me. It was clear to me that they would have a wonderful future and that we could not deprive them of this experience. He, on the other hand, could not rationalize in this way and suffered from not having them around. Occasionally I would find him in tears and would have to remind him of the fact that we must let them go, saying, "But this is much better for them! Don't you remember?"

He would immediately find his voice and say, "Of course, of course! I know that. Still, I wished our time with them hadn't gone by so quickly."

Longing for the past? I hadn't yet experienced this with him. Still, to live without the children had been difficult for both of us.

* * *

Our professional lives ran smoothly at UTD. We both taught several courses every year and were dealing with topics that seemed to be the most interesting, the most inspiring to us. During these years we published several books and articles: Pista in the field of mathematics and theoretical physics, I in the fields of literature and the Holocaust. We lived a life of deep emotional and intellectual satisfaction. I have always loved to teach, getting excited before my classes, happy to explain the variety of intellectual backgrounds and the incredibly beautiful artistic forms and relationships characterizing great literature. I loved to talk about it in my classes, and I loved to talk about it with Pista, appreciating his humor, sense of beauty, and way of looking at the world. In fact I have always seen our intellectual-spiritual attachment to one another as one of the major sources of our happiness and security. And I, who had spent the first decades of my life remembering the constant threat of murder, the yellow star, the Siege of Budapest, the new persecution, and an insurmountable fear of death, now felt that we had left it all behind. Despite missing Kathleen and Peter, I believed that our life together would continue to be ever more beautiful and bring constant fulfillment.

Yet I could not completely suppress the past or the fact of aging. That one of us might die would occur to me but only in my nightmares. Mostly, a sudden fear of the threat of death would come over me. On these occasions I would shake with fever. But if this happened at night or in my dreams, I would reach out to Pista, and immediately my fear would dissipate. If he was not lying next to me, I would call out to find him and give some other reason than fear. I did not want him to know that I was as worried about him as I was. Other times, however, when terror really took hold of me, I would tell him of my fear. He would always have a wonderful, humorous response so that I would begin to laugh and calm down immediately: "Oh yes! Of course! You have every reason to be very much afraid. I am exposed to terrible peril! Sitting in my office and reading an article about some new methods in mathematics is truly dangerous!"

But this happened just rarely. In the usual rhythm of our days, I was happy all the time, just waiting for the minute when I would see him again.

35

Threats

And then it happened. In 1998 we went on a trip to Budapest to see my brother and some of our good friends. Kathleen and Gary followed us. And while we walked from one store to another and one restaurant to the next, it became clear that Pista was not quite well: he had stomach problems. We thought this might have been caused by the "foreign food" we had been eating on the airplane. My brother prescribed all kinds of medication for him, but nothing seemed to help. Coming home to Dallas, we went to a doctor recommended to Kathleen by colleagues. We arrived at the hospital just as Dr. Simmang said that he was about to leave; in fact, it was too late for him to see Pista. But Kathleen spoke to him on the phone and convinced him to stay to examine her father. This he did and urgently recommended a colonoscopy. The next day, by the time Dr. Simmang had carried out this procedure, Kathleen arrived in Dallas. At this point we learned that Pista had colon cancer. As we returned to our car to drive home, I thought it would be better for both of us to die right there and then rather than go through the suffering that awaited us. But then after the operation, Dr. Simmang came to me and said that he had probably "gotten everything out" and that István should be doing fine within a few weeks.

The sun shone again and lit up the world. I saw the deep blue of the sky and the foamy white of the lacy clouds as we left his office. We came back to the world of living, and in the coming years I repressed the whole incident. Only late at night, in bad dreams, would I shake with fear. But then, reaching out and touching him, I would calm down immediately.

"I'm crazy," I would think on such occasions, "and it's no wonder." And then I would recall Pista's statement: "The Holocaust has frightened you for a lifetime!"

We lived on as we always had, happily, carelessly, as if life would go on forever this beautifully. Two years later a nurse and, soon after, the doctor discovered a "small" tumor on his lung. They quickly operated on him, and he was perfectly well again within a few days. I was sure that if we took care of him, nothing else could happen to us. And again I forgot this incident.

*　*　*

As before, we were teaching our classes and writing our papers and our books, but we would meet every night for our delicious supper, which we would prepare together. Later in each other's arms, again and again we would rediscover a wonderful, heavenly world. In addition to enjoying deep personal happiness, we continued to invite friends to our house on weekends and have great discussions with them around our dining table and after supper. When they left, we recalled our "Winnie the Pooh" friends in Budapest decades before and enjoyed our luck to have found such wonderful people again. Surrounded by love and friendship, guests and students, we also went to concerts and the theater and, to our great happiness, we saw our children quite often. In the meantime, Kathleen married a nice guy and a good man, and they had a beautiful daughter, Elizabeth, who has brown eyes and dark brown hair and is highly sensitive, musical, and very talented, having an exceptional inclination to the world of great literature. She also is a great skater.

Peter married as well the girl whom he loved, Shevi, and within a few years they had four little girls: Eliana, Nina, Tamar, and Leora, each of them as sweet, as beautiful, as talented, and as intelligent as the others. In fact, all of these children manifest great charm and sweetness, showing great intelligence, remarkable artistic gifts, and other talents. We have felt incredibly lucky for having them.

In the course of these years, we went to Hungary several times to visit Iván. And while earlier in my life I had always been terrified of death, the older I became, the less I thought about it, the less I felt frightened by it. Obviously, the more imminent it became, the more I suppressed it.

36

The Crush of the World

But illness rarely pays attention to our feelings and wishes. In 2013 we were hit again. Medical exams showed that Pista once again had cancer. Further studies showed that this was not a recurrence of the previous colon cancer but probably new cancer cells, and it seemed that the cancer had found its way into his liver as well.

What happened? The day before, we did not know about this. The day before, this possibility was only a nightmare, not reality—at least not for us. It had appeared only a few times, in my most frightening dreams. I had always been afraid, and I had every reason to feel this way: I was afraid about my father dying, afraid of the Germans, afraid of the Russians, afraid of the Communists, afraid of Pista's future in the field of astronomy, afraid for the children, afraid of many things; but the truth is that I had never admitted either to him or to myself my fear of his dying.

"No! He can't die!" screamed a voice inside me. "He is well! And I want to be happy with him! I want to live with him! This is a nightmare! I want to die! I want him to live!"

"No! He's not going to die," screamed another, louder one.

I lay in his arms at night as always, but now I was trembling until morning. Then I told him that everything would now change because I was going to put every part of my mind and body into the fight against his cancer.

He started to have medical treatment. At this point, however, I no longer trusted his doctors. How had they not noticed his slipping sooner? How come they did not say that he could fall sick? Where had they been? With all the developments in modern medicine, I thought they should have discovered it sooner; in fact, they should have mentioned it to us as a possibility. We thought everything was okay. Why did we only come to check twice a year? Why not three times? Why did we change, at the suggestion of the doctor, the schedule for the colonoscopy from once a year to once every two years and then to once every three years? I did not want to give in; I decided to go to another doctor. We did so and this one carried out the necessary examinations, X-rays, blood counts, and everything else. Afterward he asked to speak with both of us. The fourth person who participated in this discussion was Kathleen, who was on the other end of the speaker phone at her hospital in Albany.

The doctor was frank and clear. To Kathleen's question "What is this?" he answered without hesitation:

"Cancer that has spread from the colon to the lungs and probably from there to the liver."

"How long do you think he could live with this?" asked Kathleen—in front of all of us!

"God! Why does she ask this question? This guy's answer will ruin Pista! It will ruin me! It will ruin us! This is terrible!" a loud, desperate voice screamed within me. And then it continued, "Don't listen! You must not listen!"

But there was no hesitation to answer the question. The doctor spoke clearly and calmly: "From four months to two years."

We could not have misunderstood him. Pista's face distorted. I felt as though I was dying in this very moment. In fact, I did. Ever since that moment, I have felt that the world ended for me.

The discussion concluded. Sickened and desperate, we had nothing else to ask, nothing else to discuss. But we decided to follow his suggestions rather than stay with the previous doctor.

"What a scandalous idiot this guy is! He knows nothing!" I said as we left. "They are all idiots! Apparently, they can't constantly face death and isolate themselves from the living world. The only way they can deal with it is by interpreting this peril as part of their and everybody else's life. But you can't live with death! And neither can they! They tell the 'truth' and don't care how they hurt others! They don't care!"

I was beyond myself. Pista seemed less outraged, less angry, and less desperate; he seemed more patient, more unworried than me. I felt anger, despair, contempt, and suddenly I had nothing to hold onto. In fact, I was unwilling to consider what the doctor said; I did not want to talk about it or recall it. The next day, like me, Pista behaved as if he had forgotten the whole discussion.

He was now on new medication, and while I succeeded in suppressing my knowledge of the horrible threat his illness posed, I told myself over and over that "as he healed with his first treatment, so will he now."

Kathleen and Peter came a few times to Dallas to see him, and I asked them no questions. How would they know better than me what was happening? True, Kathleen is a doctor, but she is a vascular surgeon, not a cancer specialist. I told myself all the time that everything would turn out well because, having healed the first time, he would do it again. Sometimes, overwhelmingly paralyzing fear would rise up to quash my optimistic thoughts about his return to our house, to our life, and to our happiness, but I fought against it, reminding myself that I was infected with the unrealistic fears of my childhood. Analyzing my feelings thus, I immediately became optimistic, forcing myself to forget my anxieties. I knew they were unrealistic, based as they were on earlier traumas rather than representative of the present and the promise of good and new solutions for the future.

* * *

The front doorbell rang all the time. Friends came to visit, wanting to see and talk to both of us. But more often than not, Pista was unable to meet his visitors. He would be asleep when they came, and nobody could wake him. That worried me terribly. I could not understand why, since he would sleep throughout the night, he would be sleeping again all morning and all afternoon. And when I woke him up for lunch, why would he not want to eat, why would he rather go back to sleep than talk to me or think about mathematics? But he slept and was rarely awake during the day or night. I worried, but then I explained it to myself by saying that he must be exhausted from taking all those medications and from the great variety of treatments. All his life, he had fled from solving unbearable problems and had attempted to stay away from unpleasant circumstances. So I liked to imagine that basically, he was sleeping to get away from the problems we had to deal with. I lived with this idea for a while. Sometimes, however, I tried to discuss things with him, thinking to engage him in arguments regarding the political developments of the time, a process in which he had always been very interested. But I could not. With light smile on his lips, he would close his eyes and hold my hand.

"Where can I go? What can I do? Is he dying?" The voice started speaking inside me. "No! He isn't. He looks the same way he looked half a year ago, or four years ago, or forty years ago! He is just tortured by this whole illness, by the medications, and by the expectations he has." I began to hear and believe the voice of my father from a long time ago:

"Don't ever forget that staying in bed for a long time weakens you. Therefore, it's bad for you!"

I recognized my father's statement as being relevant to this crisis. Hence I wanted Pista to get up, to get used to the everyday world again, the world in which he had lived by now for over eight decades. Sometimes indeed he did get out of bed, but after a few minutes he would want to lie down again and immediately fell asleep.

The summer passed. He would never drive when we went somewhere together. I did all the driving. This was not because I would not let him drive but rather because he once had a small accident, and after that I drove most of the time because this was my natural impulse. But in retrospect, he never mentioned that he wanted to drive, and I never asked him about it. As a result, he did not drive. And I? I was happy about it.

"At least he's not endangering himself," I thought. Now I wish I had asked him whether or not he would like to drive sometimes, but I never did.

Then one day, I noticed that he was no longer working on his math problems.

"It's summer, and it's too hot," I told myself. "He will write again in the fall."

But he didn't. At one point he decided to read some "real literature," starting out with Thomas Mann's *Magic Mountain*. He seemed to enjoy this book very much, and we had several discussions about it. In September the doctor told us that the new medication had not helped either and that we would simply have to wait to see how some other medication would function.

I was teaching throughout the fall 2013 semester but would run home after my classes to find him mostly asleep. I was told about a new medication that might help him. He didn't look terrible, he still came shopping with me, and he was still joking all the time; in fact, he was as witty and funny as ever.

"What could happen to him," I thought. "What could happen to us? My goodness! Always, anything might happen. But it's probably not yet time. We'll probably survive! After all, we survived the Germans, we survived the Russians, we survived the bad times in Germany, we survived his first cancer, and his second. He'll be fine," I told myself, "and we'll live happily ever after."

* * *

At the beginning of November, Peter was in Dallas. He had come for a visit—probably because Kathleen had told him that the end was near. I am not sure about this, but he had come, and he was supposed to leave town on the seventh. But before going to the airport, he wanted to come with us to the doctor for a routine exam. Pista had just finished the new treatment he had been receiving for the past month and was supposed to meet the doctor in his office to discuss the results. All three of us were standing in our garage. Peter was supposed to drive when suddenly something happened that I did not immediately comprehend. Shortly after, I realized that Pista had collapsed before getting into the car. Picking him up from the floor, Peter placed him in the backseat. Peter and I sat in the front and began our rush to the doctor's office. Completely confused, I prayed, but I also tried to explain to myself what had happened.

"He ate very little yesterday, and he's exhausted because of his constant sleeping and the terrible amount of medication he's taking. No, there can't be any other reason for this fall."

Looking back in the car, I tried to see his face but could not. He was bending forward and I couldn't adjust my head. As we passed the hundreds of cars, I could think of nothing but my father's oft-told story about my then four-year-old brother Iván, who had once been critically ill. My father took him from the small town where we lived to see the doctor in Budapest. As they sat in the car driving in high traffic in a rush to the doctor's office, Iván looked around at the large number of cars. He was delighted and said excitedly, "My God, Daddy, I wish our little Zsuzsi, could see this!"

Now I thought: "My God, Peter, I wish our Iván could see this!"

After the doctor examined my brother, it turned out that Iván had tonsillitis. He was cured. I hoped and told myself again and again that Pista, too, would soon be well.

When we arrived at the doctor's office, Peter placed Pista in a wheelchair and took him into the doctor's office. In a few minutes he returned to the waiting room to say, "Dad has to stay in the hospital. That's the doctor's opinion," he added.

I went inside. The doctor came to see me.

"He doesn't seem to answer any of my questions," said the doctor. "Obviously, something's happened."

As I came out into the waiting room, I heard Peter talking with Pista in Hungarian.

"Why didn't you answer the doctor's questions?" I asked.

"Because his questions made no sense," was his answer. This was a perfectly Pista-like response. Indeed, why should he answer "stupid" questions? At any rate, he was admitted into the hospital, and I hoped we would stay there for just a little while. Then I heard with great consternation that Peter had cancelled his flight.

"But why?" I asked.

"I thought I'd stay a little longer," he replied.

Very soon, Kathleen arrived.

"What's going on?" I asked desperately, again and again. "What's going on? You're always telling me that you can't leave your office from one day to the next. Has something happened I don't know about?"

At this point, she answered very seriously, "Nothing happened that you wouldn't know about," adding the frightening statement, "except that, as you see, he is worse off than he was."

No doubt this was true. But was he not going to get better? Was he not going to heal? He was being treated with so many medications. They must help! Also, I had read in the newspaper just a few days before that there were new medications and treatments for cancer. What was Kathleen telling me? What did it mean that "he is worse off than he was?" This was not what I wanted to hear. I told myself that she was nervous and upset because on the one hand, she was worried about him and wanted to stay, while at the same time her colleagues in Albany expected her back as soon as possible. But she stayed.

"So, she is upset, feeling torn between these two places," I thought. "And that's completely understandable."

The days went by. He was asleep most of the time. Friends came to visit him, and he sometimes even talked with them.

I either stayed in the hospital for the night while Kathleen went home, or she stayed and I went home. Pista slept more and more. I wanted him to get up at least once or twice a day. He did so a few times, and he walked across the corridor—but there was no question about "going home." When I asked the doctor, he gave me only indirect answers.

The names of his various medications were listed on a blackboard in his room. One day I noticed that there was only one word on the list: morphine.

"For heaven's sake," I said to the doctor when he came in, "why is he getting morphine? Won't he heal without it? Isn't morphine addictive? What will happen when he is released from the hospital and allowed to return home? Isn't there a danger that he will become dependent on it?"

"This is not our major concern," answered the doctor coldly as he left.

"So what is our major concern?" I asked myself. "What should it be? And why is he so rude?"

I did not dare mention this discussion to Kathleen, as she, too, was behaving somewhat strangely. I noticed that Peter was avoiding staying alone with me as well. And Pista did not talk much to me—or to anybody else. I constantly tried to convince him to eat, telling him that we could go home as soon as he did. Did he believe me? I do not know.

One day before I went to bed, I noticed that his skin had a slight yellow tinge.

"Oh my God!" I thought and asked the nurse, "Does he now have hepatitis as well?"

"No," was her answer, "he'll be okay."

That night Kathleen stayed with me in the hospital. We kissed him goodnight and fell asleep.

* * *

"Oh my goodness!" We woke up to the nurse's voice. "I think he has taken his last breath."

He had. I looked at the clock on the wall. It was November 17, 4:35 A.M.

37

Life with and without Pista

Yes. He died, and we buried him. And I? I still can't fathom it. I just can't. Why did he die? Hadn't his health been improving? Did he really have cancer? Have we lost one another forever? Will I not see him ever again? Ever? Only in my dreams? And when I am awake, will I have to imagine him? Will I not see him? Will he not come home? Will I have to imagine his face? Which one? His young, boyishly open face with his high forehead? His sweet, more mature one? His intelligent, aging look? His funny nose? His beautiful, loving eyes? His light brown hair? His graying hair? His silver hair? Which one? All of them? He is all of this together. And shall I not hear his beloved voice anymore? God! But if I want, I can still hear him speak right now. Perhaps I cannot really hear it, but I imagine that I can. And wait a minute! He won't hug me anymore? He won't tell me how much he loves me? How beautiful I am? How lovely? That he has never seen anybody like me? And how good I am to have given him the children? Is it possible that he knows nothing about our life any more, and about what we have gone through together? Are there still witnesses to our beginnings?

Although my brother and my sister-in-law knew him quite well, we lived with them in Budapest for just for a little while. Later, they were not allowed to leave Hungary. After seven or eight years of separation, we finally met in Vienna, and then we met again and again, perhaps once every two or three years. But they did not know him throughout his life. They did not know his habits, his talents, his goodness, his generosity, his intelligence, his humor, and the depth of his love. They did not *really* know him. Even among our friends, there are just a few still alive who were close to Pista from the beginning, who knew him intimately. But I knew him, and I remember everything. I remember every minute of the sixty-four years we spent together. And now, I cannot fathom what happened. Have I lost my husband, my best friend? My father called him his "second son." The father of my children, my lover, my closest companion, my own body, my own soul? It can't be. He must be out shopping and will be home in just a few minutes. Oh, someone rings the doorbell! Has he come home? Did he leave his keys here? Where is he? Does he live now only in my soul? That cannot be! This is just a nightmare!

But he has not come home, and I must live with the awareness of his death despite my sense of his constant presence. He is not here; he does not talk to me; he does not wait for me in the kitchen at night when I arrive home from my last class at 10:15 P.M. As I open the garage, now I know that he won't be standing with open arms at the kitchen door; I know that he isn't around. Yet sometimes I feel his arms even though I know that I am just imagining it. I know that when the telephone rings and I pick it up, he is not going to ask, "Where is Kathleen? Where is Peter?" I hear his voice. But he is not tasting my chocolate cake, and I don't see him swooning as he eats it!

Still, lying in my bed at night, I often hear him arriving, and I wait for him to take me in his arms as soon as he enters the room. Sometimes I realize that I have only been dreaming about this, but despite this awareness I look around and feel that he is coming. I see him coming in, I hear his breath I wait for his arms, but then—I cannot feel him!

Sometimes I think back to our time in Germany. During the period of my collapse, he tried so desperately to stand by me, to give me strength, to show his love, to prove that no matter what he would never leave me, but I was so disturbed that I could think of nothing but myself and my own "crime" of having left my parents. He tried everything: he loved me every minute in every situation, every hour of the day. He shopped and cooked; he cleaned the apartment in which we lived; he took me everywhere he thought I would like to go. He talked to me about himself, about his fears and about his strengths, about his love for me, about our life, about his work, and about his view of our beautiful future. But I could think of nothing but myself, my own compulsion to go back to Hungary, thinking that otherwise my parents would die. Suppressing both the reality of my own role in our leaving Hungary and the consequences of our return, I did not consider that such a decision would make both sets of our parents desperately ill and ruin us, too.

But after a while, I started to live again. I faced up to the possibly horrific consequences of our return and to the fact that it would not help anybody and only cause harm if we did. At the same time I recognized that we had a wonderful future, which might offer us and our parents a beautiful and productive life. Also, I came to understand that while my healing had been in many ways the result of Dr. Cohen's help in Hamburg, it was in fact Pista himself whose caring, selfless love was instrumental in my coming to terms with my problems. In addition, as soon as I recovered I started to understand not only the reasons for my pangs of conscience regarding my parents but also my love for István and my duty to him as well as to our deep, lasting, miraculously loving relationship and our future! In fact, allowing myself to love him passionately again, I started to understand the reasons for my despair and started to live with him again in a heavenly universe the likes of which I had never known before. The clouds that threatened our happiness for five months in Germany created by my dark vision of myself, my compulsive belief in the need to return, and the danger threatening us all disappeared from our life completely. I started to see more clearly and lived with Pista for fifty-one more years in sublime happiness.

But now? What happens now? Is he gone? Forever? And where did he go? How can I live in this world without him? How can I survive without him?

In fact, is it worthwhile to live at all? Is it? Of course, I have my two beloved children. But life goes on, and they will survive, thank goodness, whether I die a natural or self-inflicted death. But could I do that to them? And what would he say if he were alive? Oh, he would give his life for me; he wouldn't want me to go after him. At any rate, he must be relieved right now, knowing that I turned my back on these destructive thoughts. My goodness! What was I thinking? What was I talking about? Kathleen has a daughter, and Peter has four little girls. How could I leave them? How could I do that to everybody?

I must live. This is what he would want me to do. This is what I was obliged to do as soon as I brought children into this world. But what about him? Why did he die? And how can I live without him? I haven't lived without him since I was seventeen years old, which means that I have almost never lived without him. How on earth could I learn to do so now? I cannot. He is with me in every moment of my life: when I am writing, when I am studying, when I am reading, when I am driving, when I go to sleep. I feel him even though I am just hugging and loving an imaginary figure. Perhaps I am seeing him, despite his unearthly appearance.

Sometimes when I go to teach at the university, I hope for a miraculous meeting with him—as we often met coincidentally in the past. In fact, at night he would often wait for me in the parking lot. Now it is only when I get into my car that I have to admit it: he isn't here. How can I go on living like that? Perhaps I will learn to see the present as a part of my past and the past as a part of my present. Perhaps I must allow reality to take over, demonstrating that what happened in the past is basically what is happening now since it is so difficult to distinguish between the two. My past lives in me so intensely that I feel as if it is happening today, and what is taking place today is part of that past. What I mean, perhaps, is that these two different epochs cannot be separated one from another. So what else can I do except go on and live with this sense of a dual reality in my life? I owe it to him, to our children, to others in our family, to our friends, and to everyone I have ever loved: to carry on, with him in my heart, for as long as I live.

I will try to fulfill this duty of love. I will try, Pista. I will try.

Index

A
Adenauer, Konrad, 104
Ady, Endre, 28, 140
Albany Medical School, 143
Allende, Juan, 118
anti-Jewish laws, 9, 63, 108, 134
Arany, János, 28, 66, 139
　Toldy, 139
Attila, József, 28, 144
Auschwitz, 9–10, 19–21, 64, 91, 103, 109–110

B
Babi Yar, 47
Bach, Johann Sebastian, 74, 91, 136–137
Balázs, Julia, 52
Balogh, Károly, 85, 88, 94
Baltic countries, 36–37
Baylor Hospital, 129
BBC, 79–80, 82
Beethoven, Ludwig van, 14, 22, 91, 137–138
Békéscsaba, 9, 129
Béla Bartók School of Music, 2, 5, 12, 36, 43, 65, 67, 73, 95
Berkner, Lloyd, 121
Berlin Wall, 112
Bichteler, Klaus, 117, 122
Budapest University, 12–13, 17
Budapest, Siege of, 2, 6–7, 11, 23, 29, 33–34, 57, 59, 62, 65, 69, 83, 95, 130, 134, 148
Busse, Walter, 118

C
Cohen, Michael, 122
Cold War, 104
Communist government of Hungary (Hungarian Communist Party), 1, 3–7, 15–16, 26–27, 47, 50, 54–55, 71–73, 80–81, 111
concentration camps, 31, 47, 64, 103
Connally, John Bowden, 125

D
Dallas Youth Orchestra, 136, 139
Dante Alighieri, 28
Danube River, 18, 109–110
"decorated Jew" status, 9
dehumanization, 10
Depression of 1929, 26
Detre, László, 50, 52, 90
Dickvoss, Dr., 98, 100
Dobi, István, 3

E
École Normale Supérieure, 12
Ehlers, Jürgen, 119, 122, 131
Einstein, Albert, 106
"enemies of the people" status, 2, 6, 27, 31, 49, 67, 69
Emory University, 142–143, 146
Eötvös József College, 12–16, 19–22, 50, 52
Eötvös Loránd University, 48, 145
Erdmann, Eduard, 100
ESSO, 116
"Exact Solutions of Einstein's Field," 106

F
Faragó, György, 2
Fejér, Lipót, 48

Földes, István, 49–51
Franz Liszt Music Academy, 2, 57, 64

G
Germany, 2–3, 6, 9, 18, 20, 29–32, 43, 50, 53–54, 58, 62–64, 69–71, 78, 83, 90–92, 100–104, 106–111, 113–115, 118, 122, 132, 151, 154, 159–160
Goethe, Johann Wolfgang von, 28, 91, 119, 134, 144
Graduate Research Center of the Southwest, x, 13, 121, 135, 144. *See also* University of Texas at Dallas
Grass, Günther, 118
Grimm, Brothers, ix, 91
Gyönk, 19–20, 28
Győr, 94

H
Hamburg Academy of Music, 100
Hamburg Observatory (Bergedorf), 91–92, 96, 98, 100–102, 104–107, 112, 114, 117, 145
Harvard University, 13
Heckmann, Otto, 100, 107
Herczeg, Tibor, 50–53, 88–90, 96
Hitler-Jugend (Hitler Youth), 103
Hitler, Adolf, 26, 102–103, 108–109
Holocaust Studies Program at UTD (Ackerman Center), v, xii, 144
Horthy, Miklós, 2, 31, 63, 109–110
Horváth, Zoltán, 18
Hungarian Academy of Sciences, 12
Hungarian Revolution of 1956, 80–81, 83, 85, 89, 112
Husum, 104

I
Izsák, Imre, 13, 52

J
Jahnn, Hans-Henny, 118
Jahnn, Signe, 118
Jewish Anti-Fascist Association (JAC), 32
Jewish Hospital in Budapest, 48
Johnson, Eric, 121
Jonsson, J. Erik, 125
Jordan, Pascual (Jordan Seminar), 107, 122

K
Károlyházy, Frigyes, 13
Keats, John, 140
Kennedy, JFK, 124–126
Kerr, Roy, 119

Kindertransport, x
Kistarcsa, 64
Kodály, Zoltán, 73
Kölesd, 19, 21, 25–27, 34–35, 39–42, 105
Kővári, Tamás, 13
kulak, 27, 32, 49, 69, 86
Kun, Béla, 2, 53

L
Lipták, Tamás, 13
Literary Journal (*Irodalmi Ujság*), 79

M
Mach, Ernst, 106
Mann, Thomas, 119, 134, 154
Marshall, L. C., 122
Marxism-Leninism, 52
May Day (International Workers' Day), 1, 3–4
Mengele, Josef, 10
Mindszenty, József, 47
Minkowski, Hermann, 106
Mozart, Wolfgang Amadeus, 137–138

N
Nagy, Ferenc, 80
National Science Foundation, 121
Nee'man, Yuval, 122
Neuengamme, 103

P
Pál, László, 13
Pale of Settlement, 53, 91
Palestine, 12, 110
Peenemünde, 107
Penrose, Roger, 119, 122, 131
Péter Pázmány University of Budapest, 1, 28
Petőfi, Sándor, 28, 80, 140
Phylaxia, 33–34
Pirani, Felix, 106
Princeton University, 121, 143–144
    Institute for Advanced Studies, 121

R
Radnóti, Miklós, 28, 140, 144
Rajk, László, 47
Rákosi, Mátyás, 3, 5, 79–80
Recsk (internment camp), 6
Rehder, Helmuth, 119
relativity, 106–107, 117, 119, 121, 127, 134, 145
"relativity" group, x–xi
Rényi, Alfréd, 48
Riemannian geometry, 145

Riesz, Frigyes, 48
Rindler, Wolfgang, x, 122, 124
Robinson, Ivor, x, 121, 124, 131
Rodriguez, Robert, 139
Romanian troops, 2
Roosevelt, Franklin, 109

S
Sanders, Rino, 118
Schild, Alfred, 119
Schiller, Friedrich, 28, 91, 119, 134
Schubert, Franz Peter, 91
Schücking, Engelbert, 104, 106–107, 112, 117, 119–121, 131, 145
Schumann, Robert, 91
Schuster, Emil, 117
Sebők, György, 43, 61, 65–66, 112
Shakespeare, William, 140
Shelley, Percy Bysshe, 140
Social Democratic Party, 31, 102
Southwestern Medical School, 131, 143
Soviet Union, 1–7, 12, 15, 18, 20, 24, 26–27, 29, 31–32, 36–37, 43, 45, 47–48, 51–54, 57–58, 62, 74, 76–81, 83–84, 89, 91–93, 109–111, 115, 117, 123, 129, 135, 146, 151, 154
Stalin, Josef, 2–7, 25–26, 32, 43, 47–48, 51, 54, 74, 79, 111
Stanford University, 143, 146
Syracuse University, 117, 121
Szabadka, 134

Szabadság-hegy, 50
Szabolcsi, Bence, 63–64

T
Texas Instruments, 121
Tisza River, 109
Tito, Josip Broz, 74
Trade Mart, 124–125
Trianon Conference, xii, 25
Trümper, Manfred, 122
Turán, Pál, 48
Turkish occupation (16th century), 24
Turner, Frederick (UT Dallas), 119
Ukraine, 109
University of Texas at Dallas, v, x–xii, 122, 135, 139, 143–144, 147
Voice of America, 79–80, 82

W
Wachmann, Murray, 100, 102–103, 118
Weill Cornell Medical College, 143
White Cross Hospital, 6
White Terror, 2
World War I, 3, 9, 25–26, 54, 108, 129
World War II, ix–x, 2–4, 24–26, 31–32, 52, 57, 89, 117
Yalta, Treaty of, 3
Yugoslavia, 74, 108–109

Z
Zacher, Gerd, 118

www.ingramcontent.com/pod-product-compliance
Lightning Source LLC
Chambersburg PA
CBHW070613170426
43200CB00012B/2682